Prai

MW01505771

"The perfect blueprint for anyone looking to build a portfolio of high ROI vacation rental investments, with tactical advice and real-world examples. Following Culin's advice, we've purchased over 20 properties in the past two years — and are outperforming 95% of our peers!"

TONY CAPPAERT
CEO, Blue Maple vacation rental investment fund

"Finally! A fast-moving book with detailed systems and tools to succeed in every step of short-term rental investing. If you've ever wondered how to achieve financial freedom via Airbnb, this wonderful, well-researched book tells you how to get there.

MARGOT MACHOL BISNOW
Author, *Raising an Entrepreneur* and former chief of staff,
Presidents Council of Economic Advisers

"Culin is a true short-term rental expert. Host Coach is brimming with advice, systems, and tools that I have used to increase revenue and decrease wasted time across my property portfolio. This book will absolutely take you to the next level of Airbnb hosting."

LADD GASPAROVIC
Operating Principal at Keller Williams Wilmington and Myrtle Beach, NC

"Started reading it this evening, and I can't put it down! Storytelling, facts, genuine - this is an MBA level case study wrapped in HGTV style and served at the most relevant time."

TEA WILLIAMS
Senior Business Executive, Technology Enthusiast

"If you're looking for a clear, practical guide to building financial freedom through Airbnb investing, look no further! The easy-to-apply systems provide a blueprint for building wealth on your own terms."

LAURA CANNON

Author, *The Conscious Entrepreneur*

"Culin and Danielle give new and experienced real estate investors a comprehensive insider's guide packed with valuable insights. Host Coach provides exciting and actionable strategies to crack the code for success and profitability in the short-term rental business."

DR. MARTA WILSON

Best-selling author, *LEAP*
and *CEO, Transformation Systems*

"This book is a high-quality education into the world of short-term rentals. Whether you're an experienced real estate pro, or a side-hustler looking to build up financial freedom, this book covers what you'll need for growing a fun & profitable vacation rental business."

KELVIN MAH

Founder, CEO, Rankbreeze

"Culin and Danielle have nailed the opportunity recognition with the Airbnb model in this book. Opportunity recognition serves as an integrated part of the entrepreneurial mindset. A must read for budding and serial entrepreneurs."

JOHN ZUKNICK

Director of Economic Development at Universities at Shady Grove,
Adjunct Faculty Entrepreneurship at University of Baltimore

CULIN TATE & DANIELLE TATE

HOST COACH

A Blueprint for Creating
FINANCIAL FREEDOM
Through Short-Term Rental Investing

Ten:Eleven Press

Host Coach: A Blueprint for creating financial freedom
through short-term real estate investing

Culin Tate and Danielle Tate

Copy editor: Nicole Hall
Editor: Brin Stevens
Author Photo: Carson McRae
Cover and Interior Design: Vanessa Mendozzi

Learn more from the Host Coach at www.hostcoach.co

First edition published February 1, 2022 in the United States of America
By Ten:Eleven Press

ISBN: 978-0-9970074-1-1

This book is dedicated to **you**—the courageous reader who has already taken the first step toward life-changing financial freedom by reading this book. You are holding in your hands the answers to short-term rental success.

We could not be more excited for you to start your journey!

Culin Tate is a serial entrepreneur, owner and host of eight Airbnb properties, Airbnb ambassador, short-term rental coach, and speaker. His mission is to share his experience, knowledge of specific tools and software, and the systems he has created to harness the unique opportunity of short-term rental investing so that you can enjoy a life of financial freedom to live your *why*. Learn more about his offerings for speaking, workshops, and individual coaching sessions at www.hostcoach.co.

Danielle Tate is an entrepreneur, author, Airbnb host, and Airbnb design consultant. She and Culin combined their individual talents to build a thriving Airbnb business. She now facilitates Host Coach workshops and offers individual coaching to help individuals creatively decorate their short-term rentals and repurpose property atrocities into amenities.

Also by Danielle: *Elegant Entrepreneur: The Female Founder's Guide to Starting and Growing Your First Company*

CONTENTS

Your life does not get better by chance.
It gets better by change.

— Jim Rohn

INTRODUCTION

Where are the deals?

Did you grow up with a friend whose family had a vacation home at the beach, lake, or river? Did you go there for the weekend and have an amazing experience only to find out that someone in the family bought the place for $42,000? This exact scenario happened to me several times in high school.

After graduating from college and starting my first company, I started thinking, "Where are those real estate deals for my generation? Are we ever going to have the opportunity to purchase a property for $42,000 and watch it appreciate to $420,000?"

I spent twenty-plus years thinking the answer to my question was no. Then, online housing rental platforms, such as Airbnb, VRBO, and Bookings, radically altered the travel and real estate markets. Suddenly, we *do* have the opportunity to make a real estate investment that has the potential to generate rapid returns and financial freedom.

My experiences and monetary gains as an investor and Airbnb host over the last six years have led me to believe that short-term rentals offer the most stable opportunity for wealth creation of the decade. A short-term rental property is a furnished, self-contained space that is rented for short periods of time as an alternative to hotel stays. This type of investment differs from long-term rentals, which are properties that are typically leased for a period of a year or longer. It is also different from multi-family rentals which are a property containing three or more dwelling units that are typically leased for periods of a year or longer. Comparing these three real estate investments, short-term rentals have the potential to generate much higher profits.

This book is written as a chronological journey in short-term real estate investing. Building from finding the inner purpose that will drive your initial investment, to implementing pricing strategies for occupancy, to reinvesting in, and scaling your portfolio. I recommend reading this book from cover to cover and refer back to certain chapters as they pertain to your current short-term rental investment journey. However, if you have already purchased an investment property and are eager to jump in, feel free to skip ahead to Chapter 4. And buckle up! This chapter begins the deep dive into my expertise, systems, and tools to maximize the wealth-generating capabilities of short-term rental investing.

Looking Around a Corner

We are living in the moment of the greatest opportunities/deals for our generation. Is it too late to invest in short-term rental property? No. This is exactly the right moment to get involved and start investing in Airbnb properties. I have seven cabins and an island condo that generate an average of $70,000 to $80,000 a month. Owning just one short-term rental property not only pays for itself, it could pay your primary mortgage and put cash in your pocket to either reinvest, make improvements, or donate to your favorite charity. Those are the facts for just *one* property.

The only limit to your growth potential is the time you want to put into your investments. Asset-based lenders are now funding short-term rental investments with little or no documentation. Short-term rental loans are based on the property's ability to generate income, not your personal income.

Cracking the Airbnb Algorithm

I am a tech entrepreneur. I have founded and sold electronic man-ufacturing companies and software companies across several industries. I sold my last company in 2018 and started to stress over what my next company would be. At age forty-eight, what was the next thing I could build to generate income?

Guess what? I didn't have to come up with a new idea! My small rental cabin was generating a pretty nice cash flow. I wondered, "What if I bought another cabin?" That summer I ended up buying three cabins. When I do something, I do it wholeheartedly. This was going to be my new business, so I had to figure out how to increase profits and scale up from an average Airbnb to a super-charged revenue-generating property. The processes I created and the tools I discovered through trial and error are game changers. They are the crux of this book.

Living with Purpose

Many years ago I was given a book, *The Greatest Gift* by Philip Van Doren Stern. It is a brief book written with the intent of helping the reader find his or her purpose in life. I wrote my purpose on the last page of that book. In writing this book, I am living my purpose. Curious what I wrote down? "My purpose is to discover my gifts and share them with the world for the glory of God." I have a gift for understanding algorithms and a gift for monetizing unique opportunities. I want to share my systems and tools with you to make your life better.

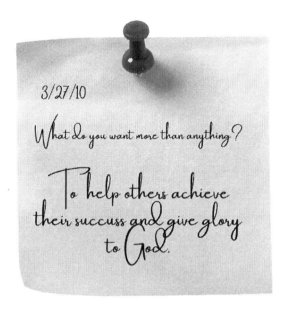

My wife and business partner, Danielle and I wish we could both personally help you. However, there are only two of us and 7,800,000,000 people on the planet. To accomplish our goal of helping as many people as possible achieve financial freedom through short-term rental investing, we wrote this book for you. Through these pages, we will share our systems, tools, and best practices. We will coach and encourage you as you embark on your short-term rental journey. This book is about real people, real strategies, real tools, and real-life experiences. Consider it part road map, part self-help, part technology magic, part business book, and part investment bible. This is going to be exciting!

1. WHY NOW? WHY SHORT-TERM RENTALS? WHY AIRBNB?

Why Now?

Our economy is currently in the midst of transformational shifts in consumer spending, personal priorities, product sourcing, and travel. The main drivers of these changes are the millennial generation and the effects on the population stemming from the COVID-19 pandemic. Currently, 22 percent of the United States population are millennials, and their numbers are expected to peak in 2036 at 81 million people.[1]

The Influx of City Dwellers

The 2000s have seen an influx of individuals, mainly millennials, moving back into cities. Pew Research found in 2018 that 88 percent of millennials live in metropolitan areas. They typically rent urban space instead of owning it. Whether they are chasing greater work opportunities, short commutes, or simply the walkable city lifestyle, millennials are not interested in purchasing homes outside the city. According to BuildZoom, 2021 home sales ten miles outside of cities are down 50 percent from sales in the year 2000.[2]

---

1 The Brookings Institution, McKinsey & Company

2 https://www.investopedia.com/news/real-reasons-millennials-arent-buying-homes

Why do we care where millennials are living? Because where a large percentage of a population lives impacts where they travel. City dwellers are looking for the opposite of what they typically see and experience daily. They are looking for rural getaways. Knowing where this population desires to visit and vacation allows us to invest in properties accordingly. The best places for short-term rental investments are rural destinations approximately one to three hours outside of medium to large cities.

The Sharing Economy

The late 1990s ushered in the new concept of a sharing economy. A sharing economy is an economic model defined as peer-to-peer–based activities of acquiring, providing, or sharing access to goods and services that is often facilitated by a community-based, online platform. Some examples of activities generated by a sharing economy include: ridesharing, coworking, reselling of personal goods, crowdfunding, and of course, apartment and house sharing.

As with any significant economic shift, opportunities arise for those with the foresight to see the moment's potential. A sharing economy offers many benefits, including ways to monetize underutilized assets (like a getaway home), save money and resources, and provide more reasonable prices for goods, services, and space.

The first well-known company associated with the sharing economy is eBay. eBay is a platform that allows individuals to sell goods to others without owning a storefront, maintaining inventory, or hosting a website. The idea may seem commonplace now but was revolutionary when it launched in 1995.

Companies like Uber and Lyft have normalized the concept of ridesharing. Over 14 million Uber rides occur each day, and many studies show that ridesharing companies make up 65–69 percent of the gig economy.[3] These enormous numbers reflect just how much

---

3 https://makeawebsitehub.com/uber-stats

the sharing economy has changed the choices that individuals are making in the way they travel to and around the city,

Likewise, homesharing has become one of the sharing economy's largest niches. It has overturned the hotel industry's monopoly on accommodations. Between 2007 and 2009, Airbnb popularized the idea of allowing people to share space in their homes, or their entire home, with those looking for lodging in a particular city or area. As eBay is a marketplace for goods, Airbnb is a marketplace for space. Homesharing and short-term rentals have turned into a booming business mainly due to the wide variety of lodging options, locations, price points available, and easily accessible online search and booking features.

The Rise in Value of Experiences

The value of experience over ownership is on the rise. According to the Harris Report, 72 percent of millennials prefer to spend money on experiences rather than on material things. So, instead of prioritizing the purchase of luxury cars or homes, millennials are spending their money on mini getaways, vacations, concerts, and gourmet dining. This shift in allocation of spending toward experiences—and getaways in particular—plays right into the rise of the short-term rental movement.

The Airbnb platform has always been extremely popular among millennial travelers due to the unique spaces and travel experiences that millennials favor. In fact, 60 percent of all guests booked through Airbnb are millennials, with a year-over-year growth rate of 128 percent.[4]

Why Short-Term Rentals

The traditional ways and places people travel are changing. Travelers are devaluing the hotel stay experience. Personally, that devaluing

---

4 https://www.airbnbcitizen.com/wp-content/uploads/2016/08/MillennialReport.pdf

shift started for me when we became parents. Hotels are awesome until you have more than your significant other along for a trip. As soon as you have a toddler, a place that has a kitchen and two bedrooms becomes more desirable. You want the option to put the kids to bed and relax a little bit with your partner.

There has also been a universal shift toward more unique travel experiences. Most travelers do not want to stay in a cookie-cutter hotel room or resort. These shifts in preference significantly boosted the homesharing industry. Why do we care? We care about this change in travel because we can participate in it and invest in it. One can finance a $200,000 investment in a condo, a small home, or a small cabin and happily garner a share of these trends. Airbnb is going to charge us 3 percent, and we can then make $6,000 to $8,000 a month in top-line revenue on our investment.

The COVID-19 Boost

The short-term rental investment return phenomenon exists around the world. It existed before the COVID-19 pandemic. COVID-19 may have been terrible for most businesses, but it turbocharged revenue for Airbnb hosts. As people were trying to escape major metropolitan areas, we experienced a 35–40 percent boost in rates during the months after COVID-19 hit the United States. A year later, we are still experiencing long-tail elevation in nightly rates that are expected to continue for the foreseeable future.

COVID-19 changed the way people travel. Suddenly, few wanted to stay in a hotel. Few wanted to book an all-inclusive vacation, and few wanted to spend time on a cruise ship. In 2020, the hotel industry surpassed 1 billion unsold rooms for the first time in history, with room revenues down nearly 48 percent. Most people were looking for a remote, safe, getaway that they could enjoy with their family without having to wear masks or worry about distancing from other guests.[5]

5 https://str.com/press-release/str-2020-officially-worst-year-on-record-for-us-hotels

The Rise of Work-Away and "Bleisure" Trips

The COVID-19 pandemic also changed how people spend their workdays. Much of the workforce got a taste of working from home instead of commuting to the office. I started receiving messages from guests saying, "Hey, my boyfriend and I decided we would both work from home. Instead of sitting in our tiny apartment in DC, we're going to book your cabin for a Tuesday and Wednesday." This "work-away" or "bleisure" (business + leisure) mentality is a game changer for weekday bookings, occupancy, and total revenue, as guests seek to combine work and play for a more enjoyable lifestyle.

Young professionals are realizing that they don't have to be at home to work from home. They can book an Airbnb, work 9:00 a.m. to 5:00 p.m., and then take a hike. This is a brand-new demand category for our listings. In the 2019 State of Travel Insurance survey, 27 percent of millennials said they took or were planning to take a mixed business/leisure trip in 2019.[6] Currently, 60 percent of US business trips turn into bleisure trips.[7] It's certain bleisure trip bookings will continue to increase as more and more guests book work-away trips and tell their friends and colleagues about their experiences.

Short-Term versus Long-Term Rental

In the early 2000s, I purchased a two-bedroom condo in Bethesda, Maryland as a rental investment. My plan was to rent the unit for a number of years, use the rent to cover the mortgage, and eventually sell the condo for a profit.

I found a long-term tenant who paid her rent for over a decade. Unfortunately, property values did not appreciate, and fifteen years later I sold the condo for the same amount of money I purchased it for. After factoring in ongoing maintenance and repair costs,

---

6 https://www.bhtp.com/blog/millennial-travel

7 https://www.stratosjets.com/blog/bleisure-travel-statistics

occasionally updating paint and carpet, and then the final costs to make the property ready for a market sale, I lost a decent amount on this "investment."

Several years later, I discovered a new investment opportunity: short-term rentals. After successfully repurposing our family cabin, I purchased an investment cabin in the Shenandoah Mountains. After furnishing and listing the cabin on Airbnb, it has consistently generated $5,000 a month in top-line revenue. So, by investing the same amount of money in a short-term rental, I have a property that generates an after-expense profit of $30,000 a year. If I had originally invested in a short-term rental instead of a long-term rental, I could have accrued $450,000 over the course of fifteen years instead of just covering a mortgage and losing money on the sale.

$450,000 is a life changing amount of money. Short-term rental investing can afford you the ability to send your children to college without debt. It can pay for your current home. It can give you the opportunity to travel the world. It can free you from a job you hate. You can use your profits to set up a charity or to take care of people in your family who are in need. Short-term rentals give you the freedom to turn your dreams into plans.

Some individuals will make the case that long-term rental investing is a passive investment. That may be the case if you employ a property management company. However, if you are running the long-term rental on your own, there are always toilets to fix, bugs to kill, and rent to chase down, along with the annual re-painting, repairing, and prepping for new tenants.

Short-term rentals are more active investments, but once you have the appropriate tools and software set up, your daily time spent on Airbnb will be ten to fifteen minutes in the morning and evening. If you enjoy hospitality, short-term rental investments are often more personally rewarding. Additionally, in my experience they produce three times the returns of long-term rental investments.

First Home versus First Short-Term Rental

Short-term rentals are changing how individuals invest their money. Instead of saving for a first home, many people are now saving for their first short-term rental down payment. Why? Instead of pouring their money into a home mortgage that provides a place to live, they are opting to invest in an asset that will generate monthly income.

Consider this: during the first quarter of 2021, the median house price in the United States was $369,000.[8] If you put down a 10 percent payment of $36,900 at 4 percent interest on a thirty-year loan, you can expect a monthly mortgage payment of $1,585 (property tax omitted.) You will have a place to live for the next thirty years, you will be accruing equity, and your home will be appreciating in value at the same rate of other homes in your market.

Alternatively, you could invest in a short-term rental property with positive cash flow. A 1,200-square foot, two-bedroom cabin can be acquired for $216,000 at $180 per square foot. Assuming the same 10 percent down payment of $21,600 and 4 percent interest on a thirty-year loan, you can expect a monthly mortgage payment of $928 (property tax omitted.) Since a short-term rental investment property costs less, you can use the difference in down payments to furnish, improve, and make your investment property ready to shine on Airbnb.

After monthly mortgage, cleaning, and expenses, this size of short-term rental investment can produce $5,000 per month in top line revenue and net a positive cash flow of $2,500 per month. This is why I say a short-term rental property will not only pay for itself, it can also pay for your primary residence and produce additional monthly cash flow.

Once you have one short-term rental investment paying for your primary living expenses, consider the financial freedom that could result from investing in one or two more properties. I truly believe that short-term rentals are the wealth building opportunity of the decade.

---

8 https://fred.stlouisfed.org/series/MSPUS

Crazy Fast Return on Investment

Traditional investments such as stocks, bonds, and primary homes can take a long time to yield results. Investments with rapid returns can seem too good to be true. Many are, but short-term rental investments are the real deal.

My friend Lou is a great guy. He owns a business and invested in a few house flips. Those investments promised fast cash, but he barely broke even. Lou noticed the success I was having with my rental cabins. Being the smart guy that he is, he started asking questions. I showed him my monthly books and he was a believer!

Lou purchased his first cabin in Hedgesville, West Virginia and allowed me to help set up his listing and apply my systems and tools. A few weeks later, I received the best text from him: "Brother, my first month's revenue from the cabin paid its mortgage and my home mortgage!" Lou's six-year-old daughter, my goddaughter, loves staying at "her" cabin; his wife enjoys managing guest relations; and he's delighted with the monthly revenue. Lou just bought his second cabin in Hedgesville to continue investing in financial freedom for his family.

My mentee Bryan has a four-bedroom beach house in Surf City, North Carolina. He purchased it, furnished it, and we worked together on his Airbnb listing. His goal was to simply cover the mortgage on the beach house. Bryan took $7,000 in bookings during the first five days his listing was published. He is now cash flowing over the mortgage amount.

Another one of my mentees, Tony, purchased a place in Berkeley Springs, West Virginia after I shared my Airbnb methodology and results with him. After his short-term rental did well, he became incredibly excited about the investment opportunity. Tony went out and raised a multimillion-dollar venture fund to purchase ten new properties. He said it was the easiest money he ever raised.

My personal experience, combined with the experiences of my mentees, makes me confident that short-term rental investing is indeed the opportunity of our generation's lifetime. This kind of investing is a vehicle to generate rapid, reliable financial returns that can lead to financial freedom for you and generations after you.

Why Airbnb

The sharing economy created the climate for Airbnb to become hugely successful. A company that started with two guys renting out air mattresses in their San Francisco apartment has scaled to a valuation of $110 billion. The Airbnb growth trajectory is something you can and should make the most of.

It is best business practice to align yourself and your investments with the proven leader in an industry. Airbnb is by far the most popular and fastest growing vacation rental platform. Airbnb currently has 5.6 million listings compared to VRBO's 2 million.[9] This ever-growing pool of rental properties around the world make Airbnb incredibly attractive to guests looking to book stays. Why wouldn't you choose the platform with the largest number of potential listings when searching for a place to stay?

On the host side, Airbnb's enormous market reach and continuous platform innovations make them the most logical choice for an investor listing a property. In November of 2021, Airbnb received 72.6 million visits. This is more than double VRBO's 33.7 million visits during the same month.[10] Since hosts make money when their property is occupied, it makes sense to for them to list on the platform with the most number of guests and the most efficient host tools.

9 Source: https://www.igms.com/airbnb-or-vrbo/

10 Source: https://www.similarweb.com/site/vrbo.com/?competitors=airbnb.com#traffic

Did you know[11],[12]:

- Every second, six guests check into an Airbnb listing.
- Since 2007, over 150 million worldwide users have booked over 800 million Airbnb stays.
- The hotel industry loses approximately $450 million in direct revenue per year to Airbnb.
- People stay an average of 2.4 times longer in Airbnbs than at hotels.
- Over 50 percent of Airbnb guests choose to stay at an Airbnb over a traditional hotel.
- Airbnb has generated $33.8 billion in revenue in the United States, to date.

Why do these facts and statistics about Airbnb matter? Airbnb is the reigning champion of the short-term rental industry. Who would you bet on in a horse race: Secretariat or some unknown thoroughbred? The safest bet is putting your money on the known winner. This mentality applies to short-term rental investing. Put your money via your listing on the biggest, most successful platform in the industry. I firmly believe in sole-platform listing with Airbnb, and will explain my rationale in detail in Chapter 7.

The Time Is Now

If you are considering investing in a short-term rental, you are not too late to capitalize on the opportunity. You are right on time. Do not wait. Do not look back in two years and think, "Man, I read a book that told me exactly how to invest and be successful. I really wish I had done that."

---

11 https://ipropertymanagement.com/research/airbnb-statistics

12 https://www.stratosjets.com/blog/airbnb-statistics

Now is the perfect time to get started in short-term rentals. In this book I will teach you things 95 percent of current hosts are not doing. For example, browse listings in your area of interest on Airbnb. Look for professional photos: there are not many. Look at listing calendars: they are not 90 percent full. Look at listing pricing; it is probably the same rate for weekdays with a slightly higher price for weekends.

This book was created to give you a set of proven systems and tools to ensure that you are the most successful host in your market and that you reap the maximum financial rewards from your investment.

→ Chapter 1 Takeaways ←

- Changes in travel and the creation of the sharing economy make now the perfect time to invest in a short-term rental.
- Short-term rental investing is the biggest wealth building opportunity of our generation's lifetime.

2. GOALS VERSUS OBSTACLES

Are you ready to set the goal of investing in a short-term rental property, or are you wavering on whether this is a good opportunity for you? If you are wavering, stop and sift through your thoughts and feelings. Now, write down all the reasons you do not think you should invest in a short-term rental. There is nothing too silly to document.

Once you have your list of reasons, weed out the self-limiting beliefs. You know, those pesky, subconscious limits that keep us from attaining our goals and living our best life.

Do any of these look familiar?

- I'm too busy to maintain a short-term rental.
- I don't have enough money to invest in a short-term rental.
- I'm not skilled enough to succeed with a short-term rental.
- I don't know where to look for a short-term rental property.
- It is too hard to find a deal in the current real estate market.
- I don't know how to set up a listing on Airbnb.
- What if I buy a place and no one books it and I lose money?
- What if I spend more money than I make?
- Are the returns on short-term rental investing too good to be true?

So many people grapple with various versions of the self-limiting beliefs listed above and with their derivatives. We all have that little voice in our head that tries to hold us back. The best way to silence the voice and move forward with your goal is to fight fear with facts.

Here are the truths to fight self-limiting beliefs:

- Short-term rental management takes less than thirty minutes per day using tools and software.
- There are myriad funding options available for short-term rental investing.
- This book will teach you exactly how to run a successful short-term rental business.
- If you enjoy spending time in destinations one to three hours from a large or medium-sized city, then these are the places to start looking for an investment property.
- If at first you do not succeed, try, try again. You only need to make one successful offer to begin your short-term rental investment journey. Don't forget, offers are free!
- Chapter 8 provides a step-by-step guide for setting up your Airbnb listing. I can also help you individually if you feel the need for a personal coach.
- If you follow the steps and strategies in this book, you will reap tremendous financial results.
- Check out the budget section in Chapter 5 to evaluate your earning potential.

After considering the facts, do you have any self-limiting beliefs remaining on your list? Cross off every item that is completely out of your control. Things like natural disasters, space invaders, and nuclear war. Hopefully, you are now looking at a list of items that are completely crossed out. If there are a few self-limiting beliefs left on your list, keep reading. We will supply the facts and systems that will quash them.

One of my life mottos comes from British writer, historian, and philosopher Thomas Carlyle.

His wise words are as follows: "Go as far as you can see; when you get there, you'll be able to see further." I have used Carlyle's wisdom to start and grow several businesses. This motto also came into play with our first short-term rental cabin.

When I purchased our family cabin in 2007, it was for personal use only. Danielle and I discussed the possibility of listing it on Airbnb, but we shared the self-limiting belief that it would only generate a few hundred dollars and would not be worth our time and effort as hosts. Wow, were we wrong.

We encouraged friends to stay at our cabin, and then friends of friends began asking to use it. The interest of strangers made us rethink our stance on offering our cabin as a short-term rental. We removed some of our personal items, took photos with a basic SLR camera, and listed the cabin on Airbnb. It was booked immediately and continuously from the first day. That was the first step in our journey as hosts and subsequent short-term rental investors.

A few years later, as I sold off the company I had been building, I had more time to play with our cabin pricing and to learn in depth about the Airbnb platform. We had professional photos taken of the cabin and increased our rates. It was amazing how much money the cabin was making and how delighted our guests were with it.

At this point my curiosity, coupled with my first cabin's revenue stream, led me to take the next step. I started looking for another cabin to purchase. While doing a walkthrough of a potential cabin with a real estate agent, I approached the owner and found she had another cabin that was not on the market. I purchased both on the spot and suddenly owned three short-term rental cabins.

We went as far as we could see with funding, beautifying, furnishing, listing, and operating our first cabin, and then we did the same with two more cabins. During this time, we were beginning to develop systems and an overall design style. We compared and tested different amenities, pricing, and policy settings between our cabins in a similar geographic location. We also built a support team of housekeepers, contractors, and landscapers. This is all possible with investment properties in multiple locations, but there can be more work associated with building out multiple support teams.

Suddenly, I could see further. I could test my algorithm and pricing theories with three properties as a data set. I began to hone my short-term rental systems and shared them with a few of my close friends who had noticed our success. I was excited to test my approach with other investors in markets outside my own. I quickly learned that my approach was teachable and repeatable as these new properties rose to the top of listing placement and generated revenue in their markets. Beyond this core group of friends, I began privately coaching individuals in different states and markets. Their unique situations, questions, and successes gave me further insights into my systems for making any Airbnb listing outperform the competition.

I went as far as I could see—again. I began to accept speaking engagements on the topic of creating financial freedom through short-term rentals. These engagements led to more coaching clients, more data, and more insights into tools, techniques, and monetization systems. Seeing further from that point, I realized we had to write a book. There are so many individuals who are curious about short-term rentals, and I wanted to create a vehicle to share my knowledge with them to help them succeed.

Everyone is nervous before they try something new. There is nothing wrong with being cautious, but do not let fear stand in the way of your success. I wrote this book with the goal of sharing how to succeed with the Airbnb arbitrage. Once you read it, you will know more than 95 percent of the hosts currently operating on the Airbnb platform.

It is incredibly easy to get bogged down by fear of what you think you do not know about short-term rentals and to then become too paralyzed to move forward. Go as far as you can see. Take the first step of identifying a market and contacting a real estate agent. I believe that you will be able to see further from there and that success is in your future.

→ Chapter 2 Takeaways ←

- Any time you make a new goal, self-limiting beliefs can creep into your mind and sow doubt. Use facts to dispel the beliefs that are holding you back from making a short-term rental investment.
- Do not get bogged down in all of the steps involved in launching a short-term rental. Take the first few steps, and then the next few steps will become more apparent and easier to accomplish.

3. FINDING YOUR SHORT-TERM RENTAL *DRIVE*

Most of us have heard about finding our *why*, but what exactly does that mean? From reading *Find Your Why* by Simon Sinek, I learned that each of us has a deep, internal *Why*. Our *Why* is our source of passion and inspiration. Happiness can come from what we do, but fulfilment comes from what drives us to do it.

What is your reason driving you to pursue a short-term rental property? You might initially think, "My *Drive* is this: I want to make a short-term rental investment so I can pay my bills." Heads up: money is not a real *Drive*. Financial freedom to travel, invest in your children's education, escape corporate America, or live differently can each be a *Drive* because each of these can be a source of passion.

What do you dream about? What idea or outcome makes your heart beat faster? What moments are you most proud of in your life? Try to crystalize the driving force or concept behind what means the most to you as a human.

It may be helpful to fill in the blanks on this *drive* statement:

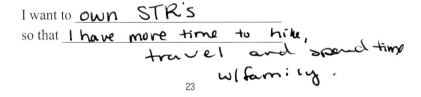

I want to own STR's
so that I have more time to hike, travel and spend time w/ family.

In this format, my *Drive* is this: "I want to use my gifts and share them with the world so that others may find success that leads to financial freedom." My internal driving force is helping others succeed. It is why I coach, speak, and wrote this book.

Why am I writing about finding your *Drive* in an investment book? Determining your *Drive* will help you overcome any fears or risks that potentially stand in the way of initiating your short-term rental investment. How you feel about what short-term rentals mean in your life is more powerful than what you think about the challenges that come with starting your investing journey. Your *Drive* is what helps you take the leap. Making an investment that allows you to live a life you are passionate about is more fulfilling than making a normal or boring investment that will yield modest returns to put in the bank.

What if you are not sure what your *Drive* is? First of all, don't worry. Short-term rental investing can be harnessed to allow you to find and live your why. By alleviating the pressures of covering all of your bills, providing for your family, and making your boss happy, you can finally have time to find and follow your *Drive*. I highly recommend reading *Finding Your Why* with your newfound financial freedom.

Short-term rental investments provide a unique opportunity to build financial freedom and live a fulfilled life. Unlike scaling other business models, like the kind I had built as a tech entrepreneur, short-term rentals remove the burden of growing a company, such as hiring and managing fifty people or inventing in a new technology. My investments gave me more freedom, and with that, an opportunity to travel. I was able to spend a "Family Study Abroad Year" in Greece in 2019. We relished the opportunity to immerse ourselves fully in a new culture, travel Europe, and grow closer together. Is this the kind of financial freedom you desire?

Short-term rentals also gave me the opportunity to be the kind of father I wanted to be. My son is a competitive lacrosse player and recently had try-outs for a better team. He had spent a year working diligently on his skills and was experiencing some nerves as try-outs approached. That is a big deal when you are twelve years old. One Monday morning, I had some work to do. I sat down in my office and started in on email but began thinking about him. As I mentally surveyed my day, I realized that I could take care of the big things that needed to be done in fifteen minutes, and then I could take the rest of the day to keep my son calm for try-outs. I was able to be present for my son when he needed me for two days, during the work week—a Monday and a Tuesday. This is a huge *Driver* for me. I have never had this level of job flexibility outside of short-term rentals. Perhaps the freedom to be present for family is what drives you.

Spending More Time in Your Favorite Place

Have you always wanted to own a getaway place but worried that it might prove too much of a financial drain? Do you envision idyllic times spent with friends or family in your favorite place? By applying the magic of short-term rental returns, you can purchase a second home for "free" and spend more time in your happy place.

What do I mean by free? You can buy a getaway home and never pay its mortgage. It does not matter if the purchase price is $216,00 or $316,000. If you are willing to rent your property on a short-term basis, even half of the time, its mortgage will be covered. If your mortgage is $926 per month or $1,361 per month, your short-term rental revenue will easily produce double those amounts.

Spending More Time with Your Family

Do you desire to spend more time with your family? Are you trying to figure out a way to make more money while remaining present for your siblings, parents, children, or grandchildren throughout their lives?

We all know we should take care not to miss the important family milestones and small moments of joy," but life is busy and full-time jobs are demanding of our time and talents. As an entrepreneur, if I did not continuously have ideas and build upon them, I would not make money. It wasn't until I started investing in short-term rentals that I broke the chains to my desk and office.

Never in my life have I had the freedom to spend a weekday on the Chesapeake Bay with my wife, take my dad to a baseball game, or devote two days to keeping my son sane during intense lacrosse try-outs. I have been able to do all of these things as a short-term rental investor. My life is fuller, and my bank account is not emptier.

My mentee Ben has a goal of purchasing three short-term rental properties. This goal is directly tied to his family. With the income from three properties, his wife can quit her job and spend more time with their seven- and ten-year-old sons. Short-term rental investing is an outstanding way to generate income without spending 9 to 5, Monday through Friday, in an office.

Diversifying Your Assets and Skills in an Ever-Changing World

The only thing guaranteed in the world is change. The changes in technology in the early 2000s were staggering. Between 2000 and the present, we saw the introduction of the iPhone, Facebook, camera phones, YouTube, Amazon Kindle and more. Those technologies dramatically disrupted the market and immediately changed desirable skills for the workforce. With such rapid and staggering advancements, it's impossible to imagine what new technologies will be introduced in the next ten, twenty, and thirty years.

Gary Beasley of RoofStock recently wrote an article for *Forbes Magazine* stating, "Investors who maintain a diversified portfolio featuring uncorrelated assets can reduce feelings of fear and anxiety during turbulent periods in the market. Incorporating real estate into an investment portfolio provides a hedge against stock market volatility. Rental properties give investors an added boost: an extra stream of income with the attractive potential for long-term growth."[13]

No matter what your investment mindset or strategy is, diversification is never a bad idea. Diversifying assets into a short-term rental gives you some protection against market volatility, stock market crashes, and even pandemics.

Career Change or Early Retirement

Are you burnt out in your current job but still need to pay your bills? Short-term rental investing is an excellent way to supplement your income while working part-time. Or, if you can invest in multiple properties, short-term rentals can completely replace your salary and allow you to retire early.

My cousin Sara is a social worker who has made the world a better place through years of hard work in unbelievably complex situations. Sara needs a break, but she also needs to pay her living expenses. She recently sold a long-term rental condo and purchased her first short-term rental in Wardensville, West Virginia. Her current plan is to use the profits from one short-term rental to fund the purchase of a second short-term rental. The revenue from two properties will fund her dream of quitting her job and moving out West with her husband to live a slower-paced life enjoying the beauty of nature.

Female-Driven Success in Short-Term Rental Investing

Did you know that approximately 55 percent of global Airbnb hosts are women? That amounts to more than 2 million women who are either investors or are employed as hosts. In a March 2021 article, Airbnb stated, "The Airbnb community is, and has always been, powered by women."[14]

---

13 https://www.forbes.com/sites/forbesrealestatecouncil/2020/01/02/real-estate-offers-a-powerful-hedge-against-market-volatility

14 https://news.airbnb.com/women-turn-to-hosting-on-airbnb-earning-over-600-million-during-pandemic

Between March of 2020 and March of 2021, new female hosts who began hosting a single listing on Airbnb since the start of the COVID-19 pandemic have collectively earned over $600 million dollars in revenue[15].

Women investors can find short-term investments more attractive than multi-family investment properties, such as duplexes and apartment buildings. Why? Danielle said it best: "I have zero desire to handle the overhead and upkeep of twenty tenants. I want the flexibility of investing in a place that I enjoy personally and that I enjoy sharing with other people." I do not know many multi-family investors that enjoy spending time in one of their apartment building units. Short-term rentals offer greater profits with more joy when compared to multi-family properties. As such, I consider them to be doubly beneficial investments.

While hosting spaces is lucrative, this is not the only way women are making money through Airbnb. Airbnb Experiences are in-person or virtual activities hosted by local experts to share their unique skills and hobbies or interesting things to do in their local. Since the launch of Online Airbnb Experiences at the beginning of the COVID-19 pandemic, 51 percent of Online Experience Hosts are women[16].

The Ultimate Host/Hostess Experience

Are you someone who delights in sharing your favorite restaurants, books, and vacation spots? Chances are you will truly derive joy from being a short-term rental host. The ultimate host loves helping guests find the perfect place to propose, identifying nature trails suitable for a two-year-old, suggesting where to surprise their mom with dinner, and providing tips on local shops to browse.

Being an attentive host will get you the 5-star reviews you

---

15 ibid.

16 Ibid.

will need to attain Superhost status the Airbnb platform—which I discuss more specifically in Chapter 11. Even if you choose to automate all of your guest messaging, receiving a 5-star review that expresses appreciation for local tips, and how special the vacation was because of these, will make you feel good. It is also good for future bookings of your listing, the local community, and the local economy. The positive, ripple effects of good people hosting good people are endless.

Creative Outlet for Design and Décor

Do you love decorating your own home? Do you have an insatiable appetite for home design shows and magazines? Is your spouse officially "over" your habit of redecorating the same rooms in your house? Short-term rentals offer a creative outlet like few others as you get a chance to totally transform an entire cottage, cabin, or bungalow.

One of our first short-term rental investments was a wood-interior log cabin, and Danielle paired a blue velvet couch with a cowhide rug in the living room. This could not be further from her transitional beach-chic design style, but it worked perfectly in the cabin. She loves creating spaces for guests that are beautiful, functional, and out of the ordinary.

Decorating an Airbnb listing affords you the fun of trying a new design style or color scheme with zero judgement. Typically, you will never meet your guests. So, you are free to wander the aisles of HomeGoods, IKEA, and your other favorite home décor stores and express your creativity!

Caregiver Side Hustle

There are many people who forgo or step back from a career in order to care for children or elders. These caregivers are essential, but they can sometimes feel underutilized. Many are looking for a job that has flexible hours and pays well. Short-term rental management offers exactly that!

We know several couples who have invested in short-term rentals. Typically, the partner who stays home runs the day-to-day operations while the children are at school or while elderly family members are napping. Both partners handle rental property upkeep on weekends while the family enjoys being in a new setting. Short-term rental investing is extremely well suited for couple teams.

Is short-term rental hosting something you can see yourself doing repeatedly, happily, and successfully? If so, this means you will feel energized by your actions as a host. You have the opportunity to live a life full of energy and passion. In this scenario, short-term rentals go beyond a revenue investment and become a long-term investment in personal happiness.

→ Chapter 3 Takeaways ←

- Understanding your *Drive* can help you overcome your fears about short-term rental investing and clarify what your goals are.
- Short-term rental investing can create financial freedom that allows you to lead a happier life.
- Short-term rentals provide income with a flexible schedule, which can be particularly attractive to women.

→ Further Reading ←

Find Your Why by Simon Sinek

4. FINDING YOUR SHORT-TERM RENTAL *WHERE*

Property Selection

My investment thesis for any short-term rental property has always been: Buy within one to three hours' driving distance of any major city, there exists a place (or places) that people like to escape to. Take a moment to consider: Where do people in your city, of your age and demographic, like to spend time? Include your friends as you brainstorm these lists. When you plan a three-day weekend trip or a romantic getaway, where do you travel? Google the best places to visit in your state. These are the areas to explore when considering an investment in a short-term rental property.

Where you enjoy going matters. Why? Because you should invest in an area where you want to spend time. It is the opposite of the multi-family investing mentality. No one I know in that investment niche ever stays in their units. Our mentality is quite different. When you invest in short-term rentals, it is important to choose a location that you will be comfortable visiting, working in, and promoting. The more pleasure you take in the location of your short-term rental investment, the easier it will be to help guests plan their stays, and the more you will enjoy working on your investment. This concept is similar to the saying, "Do what you love, and you'll never work a day in your life." In my experience, money follows energy.

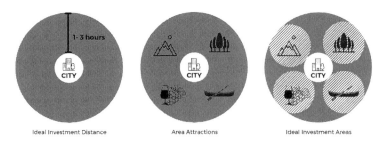

Ideal Investment Distance   Area Attractions   Ideal Investment Areas

Copyright Ten:Eleven Press

Maybe your favorite area is the mountains, a river valley, a ski location, a lake, a national forest, or wine country. Weekend getaway places in these areas make the best investments. Unlike downtown city properties, getaway locations have the potential to be scooped at a low price and repurposed into successful full-time, short-term rentals.

Another way to identify viable short-term rental investment areas is to go to the Airbnb website and enter your home city in the *Location* search box. Expand your search radius outward by zooming out on the map 100 to 200 miles and start looking for clusters of Airbnb listings. When you see 100 to 500 Airbnb listings, you know you are looking at an area worthy of investment. Areas with those listing numbers have sufficient market demand but are not overdeveloped. If you see an area with 1,000 Airbnb listings, the market may be saturated, and you may find properties that are overpriced. Ideally, cross-compare clusters with areas that you and your friends know about, have heard about, or have visited.

Pro Host Tip: Finding an up-and-coming area will give you the opportunity to purchase an investment property at a lower price than a fully established area. This is particularly helpful if you are working with a smaller budget. The sweet spot for an initial investment ranges between $150–$300 per square foot.

Once you have found a few areas with investment potential that interest you, head to Redfin.com or Realtor.com and type in the name of one of the towns in an Airbnb cluster. Then draw a circle around that area. Elect to have listings from this circle emailed to you daily. Do this for at least one other pocket of Airbnb listings you identified in your search. Receiving and scanning these emails will allow you to develop an eye for price per square foot and for the general quality of real estate in these areas. If you see a listing you like, add it to your wish list so that you can compare it with future listings as they pop up. Consider creating a spreadsheet to track the list prices, number of bedrooms, square footage, and notable amenities of these properties.

The next step is to make contact with two or three real estate agents who list places you like. You may not be ready to buy, but it is vital to establish relationships with real estate agents in the areas in which you are interested in investing. Start with a simple call or email to each agent. Introduce yourself and tell them that you are looking to make a short-term rental investment in their area. Some real estate agents will be short-term rental savvy, and others will not be as excited or interested in working with you.

Keep reaching out until you find a professional you connect with and who understands your vision and goals. Tell them you are looking for an up-and-coming area and that, ideally, you want to purchase someone's weekend getaway place. That real estate agent may suggest other areas to investigate and will begin sending you listings that match your criteria. My real estate agent, Andy, sends me at least three listings per week in a variety of areas. He knows what I like to invest in and provides an extra set of eyes as I look for potential properties.

Research Short-Term Rental Regulations

As you investigate markets and properties it is important to understand any short-term rental regulations that may apply. In this case, it is very much let the buyer beware. You, and/or your real estate agent, must check county, city, and specific Home Owner's Association (HOA) rules for properties you are considering investing in. It is better to know that a permit is required or that rentals less than 30 days are forbidden, before you fall in love and purchase a property. There are always inexpensive and gorgeous cabins popping up for sale in a certain region of Virginia. I refuse to buy them because of how difficult it is to jump through the legal hoops to operate an Airbnb in the area.

Repurposing Weekend Getaways into Short-Term Rentals

Many people purchase a house at the lake, river, or mountains, and they use it as their family weekend getaway. They enjoy the house frequently when their children are young, and then the visits taper off as school and sports encroach more and more upon weekend time. Eventually, people realize they should sell their seldom-used asset. They are selling that asset based on their use case of a family getaway home. Their agent is probably going to price the property based on that use case and local comparable sales. The real arbitrage is finding this scenario. If you are looking to maximize your investment performance, find properties being sold as family weekend getaways and repurpose that asset into a 97 percent occupied short-term rental.

To Beach or Not to Beach

Many people daydream about having a beach house; however, a place at the beach may not be an ideal short-term rental investment. Why? Because beach properties have rental income baked into their selling prices, and historically, they have the added constraint of a limited rental season.

From my discussions with beach investors, I realize that the seasonality of beach houses is changing. In the past, beach houses in the Carolinas might have had a three- or four-month rental season. We are now finding through Airbnb that investors can rent for a larger portion of the year. Given these changes, there is the possibility of generating income by buying a beach house priced for a fourteen-week season and converting it into a longer season rental. But that is not necessarily where you will find the highest return on investment.

The typical price per square foot for a rural property is $200. The price per square foot for a beachfront property or one that is one block off the beach can average $600–$800 per square foot. Could I purchase a beach house at $650 per square foot and use my methodology to cover its mortgage and throw off some revenue? Sure. But it is not an optimal investment for me.

I would prefer to buy three cabins that generate $10,000 per month in revenue, because I purchased them at $200 per square foot. The beach and/or urban settings with existing robust markets are not where I invest. I am focused on buying for maximum returns. The big boost in the return on rural investment properties is in their repurposing. You can purchase them for the price of a weekend getaway home and then repurpose these assets into full-time wealth builders that generate enormous returns. This is the investment class on which I am laser focused, and which I suggest you consider as well.

My sister has her own solution for wanting a beach house. Lisa purchased her short-term rental cabin in the Blue Ridge Mountains mainly as a new income stream. Her plan is to save that income for five years and use it to pay for a beach house to retire in. A tried-and-true strategy is to invest in assets that produce cash flow which can be reinvested into more cash flowing assets or into luxuries you desire.

AirDNA

Once you have found a few areas that interest you, it is time to evaluate their merits in terms of market demographics. There is a great software as a service (SaaS) tool for analyzing a specific market for short-term rental potential. It is called AirDNA. This software delivers critical information regarding short-term rentals in whatever region interests you. You pay per market and per month.

My friend Louis paid to analyze the Hedgesville market during his analysis phase and then cancelled his subscription after making an offer on a property. It cost him under $100 to validate that his area of interest was viable for short-term rentals.

AirDNA pulls all market information from Airbnb into its system and then generates a market analysis. The analysis provides an overall "investment grade" for an area. You will immediately see an overall grade (A+ to F) for short-term rentals in that market and a score of 1 to 100. As investors, we are hoping to see a grade between B+ and A+. This grading system breaks data into five major categories: rental demand, revenue growth, seasonality, regulation, and investability. Each category has its own score, ranging from 1 to 100.

The AirDNA Market Minder Dashboard

Image from www.airdna.co

AirDNA does a great job providing the average daily rate (ADR), occupancy rates, and overall average revenue per unit for rentals in a given market. Their data comes directly from Airbnb's Application Programming Interface (API), so you are looking at the latest twelve months of historically booked rental rates. You can filter properties by number of bedrooms to find the revenue generated by properties like the ones you are considering. I love making investment decisions based on hard data, and this tool is very helpful in determining the success of a short-term rental endeavor.

The AirDNA Market Minder Dashboard

Image from www.airdna.co

Keep in mind that ADRs are averages, and if you follow the systems outlined in this book, you can expect to significantly outperform the "average" daily rate over time. Similarly, we will be striving to outperform the average occupancy by achieving a target of 90–98 percent occupancy. This data is also very useful for creating projections of your overall profitability by taking into account your expected revenues and expected costs in a projected profit and loss statement. A pro forma profit and loss is a projection of your property's net income for a period of time.

Average Property vs. Property Priced for Occupancy Pro Forma Profit and Loss Statement

	Average 2 Bedroom	Optimized 2 Bedroom
Average Daily Rate	$189	$245
Occupancy	87%	94%
Rented Nights	26	28
Revenue	$4,914	$6,860
Mortgage (Including Taxes)	$869	$869
Cleaning Fees	$720	$720
Minor Repairs & Improvements	$300	$300
Insurance	$100	$100
Electricity	$125	$125
Internet	$106	$106
Water	$70	$70
Landscaping	$50	$50
Cleaning Supplies	$50	$50
Expenses	$2,390	$2,390
Net Income	$2,524	$4,470
Net Margin	51.36%	65.16%

Rental Seasonality is another metric to keep in mind as you look for your ideal investment market. In some markets, winter occupancy rates are lower than summer occupancy rates. As a host, you will need to compensate for your market seasonality through price adjustments. Hosts should not keep the same nightly rate year-round and be 50 percent occupied in slow months. Instead, you must lower your rates to maintain an occupancy level of 90 percent or higher at all times. This idea of pricing for occupancy allows you to generate income on maximum booked nights and also feeds the Airbnb algorithm. These concepts are covered on a deeper level in Chapter 8.

The **Investability Score** on AirDNA takes the average home sale price and compares it to the average daily Airbnb rental rate. The best short-term rental investments are in areas where the price of the home is low in comparison to the average nightly rental rate. Investments in these markets give you the maximum ratio of rental rate to house price, allowing you to achieve the greatest returns on investment (ROI).

AirDNA has many more features to explore, but I have covered the basics to prepare you for evaluating a market for investment. If you are committed to making a short-term rental investment, you will eventually be using PriceLabs to set dynamic pricing. This tool is explained in detail in Chapter 7. PriceLabs also offers a Market Dashboard tool that you can subscribe to. It offers Key Performance Indicators (KPIs) that you can utilize in your market investigation phase if you are the type of person who enjoys digging deeply into data.

PriceLabs—Market Dashboard

A second powerful tool you should utilize to evaluate the performance of a specific market is PriceLabs Market Dashboard. This is a paid tool, but it is very inexpensive and will provide you invaluable insights into the performance of the current property listings in your target market.

Let's say you are interested in a potential property and want to determine what similar properties in the area are generating in annual revenue. Go to pricelabs.co and select *Create Market Dashboard*. You will be prompted to enter a street address and radius out from that address to create a result for a competitive set of short-term rental properties. The initial results will show all active listings in the radius you have selected. Next, you will want to apply the *Bedroom* filter to view listings that have the same number of bedrooms as your property of interest.

Listing ID	Link	Bedrooms	Star Rating	Reviews	Price	Occupancy	Revenue
filter data...							
26949188	ABnB	2	5.0	3	1000	28	72510
6066667	ABnB	2	4.89	93	350	56	62790
34412987	ABnB	2	4.93	123	203	70	54532
28289300	ABnB	2	4.84	120	260	79	54061
38822432	ABnB	2	4.96	180	175	86	50955
13898085	ABnB	2	4.82	165	199	75	48939
18442568	ABnB	2	4.9	139	243	70	48915
36598370	ABnB	2	4.89	56	200	78	48725
27987592	ABnB	2	4.81	104	393	78	48554
15179072	ABnB	2	4.95	57	219	69	48187

PriceLabs Market Dashboard Report

Image from www.pricelabs.co

A complete chart of all the active listings in your radius will be generated. You can then sort by average price, occupancy, and total revenue over the past twelve months. I like to sort these results by the total revenue from highest to lowest. You can then begin clicking through the individual listings to evaluate how they compare to the property you are considering. The first few highest revenue generating properties may be unique and exceptional properties, so continue working down the list until you find properties that are equivalent in condition and amenities to your target property. This exercise will show you the exact revenue potential for your target property assuming it is managed as well as or better than the equivalent listing. The market dashboard is an oracle into the specific existing properties in the market and neighborhood that you are considering investing in.

What to Look for in a Property

Now that you have selected the area you plan to invest in and are receiving daily listings from Redfin or a similar service, you might be wondering how to select a viable short-term rental property. As you compare properties, look at their location-based and property-specific macro amenities. My loose definition of a macro amenity is a property attribute that most people do not have in their apartment or home. Location-based macro amenities include things like scenic views, river or lake access, nearby hiking trails, or proximity to a winery, ski resort, or national park.

As you begin to evaluate properties, start with their exteriors. Personally, I prefer properties that look like a cabin or possess unique architectural elements and, ideally, some beautiful views or a feeling of privacy and seclusion. Remember, guests are looking for a property to rent that is different from their personal homes or apartments.

When you look at interiors, mentally remove all of the furniture and anything big and unsightly, like wagon-wheel chandeliers or deer heads mounted on walls. Pay close attention to a property's kitchen and bathrooms. Fixtures can be replaced, and walls can be painted inexpensively. Renovations can be done either before listing your space or as a phase-two upgrade depending on your budget and timeline.

Another location-based macro amenity to be considered are neighboring houses and the neighborhood the property is in. I have looked at gorgeous cabins with breathtaking views next to broken-down trailers with piles of junk and garbage in the yard. You cannot create a 5-star guest experience if the surrounding area is scary, dirty, or dangerous. Pass on those deals, no matter how well they are priced. You will avoid endless headaches and heartaches as a host.

Property-specific macro amenities include interesting architecture, a large front porch, a fireplace, or a hot tub. They can also be a screened porch, a nice kitchen, a deck, a claw foot bathtub, game room, hardscaping, or an archery area.

> **Pro Host Tip:** Avoid investing in properties with large swimming pools. A pool can be very attractive to guests but a liability for hosts. Should guests party in the pool, unlike a hot tub, you cannot drain and refill it in 30 minutes to be ready for the new guests checking in later that day.

Crispy versus Turnkey Properties

Curious about what we consider to be the ideal condition of a short-term rental property investment? Danielle loves to buy old "crispy" cabins for a low price and then renovate them into gorgeous Airbnbs. Crispy properties are typically in somewhat poor condition and require either professional interior and/or exterior renovations (but not a gut job) before they can be listed. However, there is a significant difference between a property that is crispy and a property that is ramshackle. The benefit of buying crispy is a low purchase price. When considering this investment option, you should factor in the costs of renovations as well as the opportunity expense of not being able to list your property as quickly as possible.

Crispy cabins may appeal to those of you with endless creativity who love watching home makeover shows. Unless you, your partner, or a family member are contractors, be cautious when buying a ramshackle property; they can be money pits instead of revenue generators.

I prefer to purchase properties that do not require extensive interior or exterior work. I am happy to clean up the yard and land-scaping or repaint the exterior. I do not enjoy spending time and money on my wife's beloved crispy cabins. She sees the endless possibilities, and I see the headaches, contractor bills, and a longer lead time until listing the property on Airbnb.

Turnkey or nearly turnkey properties have the benefit of requiring minimal work before they are ready for listing and guests. With this type of investment, you can purchase, furnish, list, and immediately start making money. The downside of turnkey places can be their price tag. The more you spend on your investment, the higher your mortgage payment is, which will impact your monthly profits.

For us, the compromise is that Danielle and I both like properties that are somewhere in the middle of crispy and turnkey: places with quirks that might not make them attractive to buyers looking for a full-time residence. Danielle specializes in turning a property's worst aspects into guest amenities, and I lend my skills to make the dream a reality. Together, we make beautiful cabins.

Several years ago, we purchased a cabin with an old tool shed in the backyard. Our real estate agent recommended tearing it down, but Danielle's creative wheels were turning. She considered turning it into a yoga room or a pottery studio and finally settled on trans-forming that old shed into a garden pub.

Guests now go out of their way to book the cabin with the garden pub because it is like having their own mini pub. The garden pub features a bar, leather couch, darts, and twinkle lights. This amenity appeals to parents with young children who can go hang out when the kids are in bed as well as couples who want a cool spot to hang out without driving into town.

The best approach is to look at properties with a realistic under-standing of your own skill set and also with a creative mindset that lets you envision the possibilities for guest amenities. Balancing your skills and creativity will help you find your ideal short-term rental property.

Setting a Budget that Works for You

It is time to think about your budget. It is important to anticipate how much money you will need to invest in a short-term rental. The biggest cost will be purchasing the property. When you are looking at short-term rental investments, I like to use a rough pricing metric of $200,000 for a two-bedroom property, $300,000 for a three-bedroom property, and $400,000 for a four-bedroom property. This metric works in my market and in the majority of the secondary markets where I have mentees.

If you are making your first short-term rental investment, I would advise starting with a two-bedroom property priced in the $200,000 range. If you are buying in a popular or famous getaway market, you may pay more. Conversely, if you purchase a property in an emerging market, you may find a place for less.

If your goal for your short-term rental investment is to maximize returns, opt for the lowest mortgage payment possible. This is not a primary home you are trying to pay down: it is a cash machine. This means you want to lock in the lowest interest rate, secure a thirty-year term, and put down the lowest possible down payment. As a host, you will automatically force the appreciation of the property. Your investment in modernizing the paint and decor will increase the resale value of the property. Also, if you ever sell the property, you will sell it as an investment property with a documented cash flow stream.

It is important to work within your personal budget. It is never fun to feel overleveraged. Use the amount of cash and loans you qualify for to give yourself a ballpark number for your investment. Then add in another 2–10 percent of the purchase price to fund upgrades that will transform your place from listing quality to Airbnb beautiful.

Overpriced versus Opportunity

What happens when you find a listing you love, and it is overpriced? It is key to remember this: the whole idea of overpriced is based on the lens you are using. When my sister was looking for her first short-term rental investment, it took several conversations to get her over the concept of certain cabins or chalets being overpriced.

Adopt an investor mindset when considering property pricing. If you are looking at properties for a family getaway—a place you will visit once per month on average—price matters. If a three-bedroom cabin is historically worth $250,000 and it is currently offered at $300,000, you would see it as overpriced. It might not be a good deal for your family.

However, that cabin is only overpriced in that particular scenario. As an investor, the $300,000 cabin is not a getaway. It is an investment with the potential to generate over $10,000 in monthly revenue and $120,000 in annual revenue. Looking at it from that lens, is it overpriced? No! It is not overpriced; it is an opportunity!

Post-Purchase Costs

Every rental property is different, but we believe strongly in the juxtaposition of a rustic or interesting exterior and a contemporary interior. You as the investor will set your update budget based on what you have to spend. We see investor budgets that fall into the spectrum of lower (1–2 percent of purchase price), moderate (5 percent of purchase price), and high (10 percent of purchase price) for post-purchase upgrades. Choose the one that works best for your situation.

Make a list of all the changes you would like to make to your investment property. Then, prioritize that list in terms of Must Do items and Would Like to Do items. Determine your budget and use it to accomplish the highest priority projects or purchases on your list. Word to the wise: you should know that this list never ends.

Post-Purchase Upgrade Budget Categories

- Minor do-it-yourself cosmetic fixes
- Interior and/or exterior paint
- Indoor and outdoor furniture

- Household goods and decor
- Linens
- Landscaping
- Flooring
- Kitchen and bathroom renovations
- Macro amenities—hot tubs, decks, hardscaping

Lower Upgrade Budget

If your short-term rental down payment is consuming all of the funds you have earmarked, you can absolutely make minimal changes and list your property on Airbnb. A lower upgrade budget for a $200,000 property would range from $2,000–$4,000. In this scenario, investors typically save a percentage of their revenue after the listing is active and cash flowing for future upgrades to the property and furnishings.

A great deal can be accomplished with creativity, thriftiness, and sweat equity. Simply removing clutter and deep cleaning a place can make a huge difference. Swapping out old curtains for white panels is an inexpensive and instant upgrade. Painting an accent wall yourself costs $20 and makes a huge visual impact in photos. Consider searching Facebook Marketplace for outdoor furniture that you can spray-paint and place on the porch. If you choose to keep beds and couches that convey with your purchase, you can replace duvet covers and use slip covers to neutralize and modernize.

Moderate Upgrade Budget

If your property requires more significant upgrades that place you in the range of moderate upgrade budget, plan on purchasing all new furniture, painting all interior walls, and replacing outdated light fixtures. Typically, in this scenario, you are repurposing an old cabin or an outdated bungalow. Donate all of the old decor and start fresh.

A moderate upgrade budget of $10,000 for a $200,000 property will help you take your rental from dead animals and doilies to clean and crisp. This number gives you room to really transform a place. I love investing in properties like this because we can prepare them for listing in less than two weeks and begin generating revenue.

In our moderate upgrade plans we make all of the top priority changes we can for $10,000, and we immediately list the property. We then plan for, save for, and schedule additional upgrades from the cash flow of the cabin. These additional upgrades usually include decks, hot tubs, nicer countertops, and upgraded flooring.

Full Upgrade Budget

Some investors prefer doing all repairs, renovations, and upgrades on their properties before they list them. A full upgrade budget for a $200,000 property is $20,000 or more. My friend Louis renovated both bathrooms in his first cabin before listing, and my client Mike gutted and redid the majority of his second investment cabin before putting it on the Airbnb platform.

The major benefit of completely upgrading your short-term rental property before listing is that you have the best possible version of the property to share with your guests. You are able to charge higher prices and receive rave guest reviews. The downsides of complete upgrades are the costs of renovations, the hassle of managing contractors, and the time delay in listing your property.

Short-term rental investing is a personal journey. There are overarching constructs to follow for success, but you must do what is best for your budget, expectations, and lifestyle. As long as you commit to continuous improvement of your property, you will prosper.

Finding Deals That Do Not Exist

The deals are out there. As a potential investor, you should not be thinking, "I can't find a listing." If there are not any listings in the town in which you want to invest, go find one. If you want to be in a rural mountain area, talk to the local real estate agents and personally work to dig up some deals. Leverage your passion for financial freedom to fuel your search.

Do not be afraid to use creative tactics. More than half of the properties I have purchased were off-market deals. I have purchased directly from individuals whom I have propositioned. I have worked with a wholesaler. I have also sent email and letter campaigns to neighborhoods we were looking to invest in. If you are motivated and dedicated, you will find a property.

Off-Market Deals

To date, I have purchased three off-market properties for my investment portfolio. An off-market property is any property that is not listed on a public listing service, such as the MLS. This category can include for sale by owner or even properties that are not for sale. I find the best way to identify these properties is by getting to know your neighbors and making it known in the community that you are actively looking to purchase additional real estate.

Maintaining relationships with local service providers and amenity providers in my market has resulted in referrals to potential sellers. In one case, I was purchasing a home from a seller and realized that she owned a second unlisted property. I made her a cash offer for her second cabin and highlighted the benefit that she would not need to pay broker commissions. My offer was accepted, and that cabin grosses $100,000 annually.

I make a point of treating sellers very well during real estate transactions, which can include making some concessions in their favor. My seller relationships have led to several other off-market opportunities. Seller relationships may take time and effort to cultivate, but they have the potential to pay large dividends over time. It may be tough to get started in real estate investing, but once you dive in and gain momentum, deals and opportunities begin to find you!

Working With Wholesalers

Curious as to how you find a wholesaler in your market? Be on the lookout for signs that say, *We Buy Ugly Houses*. These signs are typically used by wholesalers looking to purchase distressed properties and sell them to investors. Call the number on the sign and start a conversation with the wholesaler. Ask them what they are looking for, and then tell them what you are looking for. Often, a wholesaler does not want what you are looking for but will keep an eye out for you.

Our wholesaler experience was both unexpected and interesting. Danielle received a voicemail from a person interested in buying our first cabin. The message said, "I see you have a cabin that is non-owner occupied. Would you be interested in selling it?"

We obviously did not want to sell our cabin, but I was curious as to how this guy got our number and what he was up to. I checked out his website and saw that he was a wholesaler. So I gave him a call. Our conversation went something like this: "Hey Paul, I am not really interested in selling my cabin, but I can tell that you are a wholesaler and that you are working in my area. I am looking for any property that looks like a cabin. Could you please put me on your investor list?"

Paul and I chatted a bit more about what each of us was looking for and hung up. Two weeks later, Paul called me about a four-bedroom cabin on top of a mountain in Shenandoah. It was in terrible condition. In fact, it had been a treatment home for troubled teens at one point. But it had breathtaking panoramic views. I purchased it for $180,000 and then invested another $100,000 in a driveway, a well, and renovations. That cabin is now bringing in $125,000 in revenue per year. It is one of the top-performing properties in my portfolio.

I would never have found that cabin on my own and had the opportunity to turn it into a revenue generating machine. One call to a wholesaler opened the door to not only a deal, but to a real estate colleague and friend.

It is always best to be prepared to act quickly when making offers on a house. It is even more important to be prepared when working with a wholesaler, as they will be offering the property to a list of investors that they have developed for many years. The wholesaler may require a larger non-refundable deposit and be less interested in contingencies than a traditional on-market sale. You can increase your odds of finding an off-market property by getting on as many wholesaler lists as possible.

Freestyling

Another way to find unlisted deals is to "freestyle." Danielle and I love to drive through winding roads in our investment areas and try to spot *For Sale By Owner* signs. Even if you don't end up purchasing a property from your exploration, you will become more familiar with your market. You will know which roads or neighborhoods are most desirable when a listing does pop up.

Be a brave investor. Fortune favors the bold. Cold-call agents and wholesalers, freestyle, send emails or written notes to the owners of properties you like. The creative and resilient investor can come up with a deal, even in the toughest of markets.

→ Chapter 4 Takeaways ←

- Within one to three hours of any major metropolitan city exist getaway regions that make ideal short-term rental locations.
- Repurposing weekend getaway homes into high-occupancy short-term rentals is an outstanding way to generate monthly revenue to build financial freedom.
- Look for macro amenities when deciding on your short-term rental purchase.
- Include post purchase costs and upgrades in your initial investment budget.

→ Tools & Resources ←

AirDNA is a software that uses information from Airbnb to generate a market analysis and overall investment grade for a specific market.

Pricelabs is a fully automated personalized dashboard to track vacation rental and Airbnb data in any market.

→ Have Questions or Need Help? ←

If you have questions or concerns at this point, please email me at **questions@hostcoach.co**

5. FINDING FUNDING AND EVALUATING RETURNS

My best advice for new investors is to secure your financing before you begin actively looking for a short-term rental investment. The worst feeling as an investor is to find your perfect place and then lose it because you were not ready when another buyer was. There are a multitude of traditional and non-traditional funding options available. These funding options are rapidly shifting and fluctuating. Presented here is a brief overview of options that may work for you.

Personal Savings

Achieving financial freedom begins with establishing the habit of saving. It is often said that if you cannot learn to save when you are making small amounts of money, making more money will not improve your ability to save. If you do not have a clear plan for your savings, it can be psychologically difficult to put away money. When your brain asks, "What are we saving for?" you need to have a prompt response.

Creating an investment goal for your savings that will yield a high cash flow can make controlling your spending easier. Consider the benefits of leverage to help provide personal motivation. If you can save enough for the down payment ($20,000) on a short-term rental property, these savings can be used to acquire and prepare your property. It is very feasible that property will net a positive cash flow in the range of $2,000 to $4,000 per month, after expenses.

Many investment and real estate professionals will advise you to invest in cash-flowing assets that will fund your luxuries. In other words, your assets should pay for your lifestyle. You must start by saving capital to make this investment. Once you begin saving, it becomes far less difficult. You might even find yourself making a game of it—how frugal can you be to boost savings for your investment?

"Start your purse to jingling." This is a directive from one of my favorite investment books, *The Richest Man in Babylon* by George S. Clason. What does it mean? Make saving automatic. Create a savings account dedicated to acquiring your investment start-up capital. Then set up automatic, weekly deposits from your primary income account. If money from your paycheck goes into your investment account automatically, you will never miss the funds. Understanding that you can leverage that saved capital into a life-changing cash flow stream from your short-term rental investment will spur you to find new ways to cut back on frivolous spending and pour more money into savings.

Friends and Family

Consider the possibility of borrowing investment capital from friends and family. You can expect their first question to be the following: "What do you need the money for?" Armed with this book as a guide, you will have identified a market, researched area rental returns, and created a firm plan with which you can present your short-term investment goals. Additionally, you should propose when and how you will repay borrowed funds. If your friends and family are not ready, willing, or able to help you today, at least you know that you fully explored this option to accelerate your path to financial freedom.

Full Cash Offer

"Cash is king" is a phrase popularized by the CEO of Volvo, Pehr G. Gyllenhammar, after the 1987 stock market crash. When it comes to real estate deals, cash is truly king. If you have enough cash saved to cover your first short-term rental property purchase, you have a distinct advantage. Sellers love cash offers, as they present less risk to the seller.

Banks often take a long time to process loan applications through their underwriting process. They are also beholden to the schedules of third-party appraisal companies. In competitive buying markets where a seller is expecting multiple offers on their property, cash offers will generally win the deal over non-cash offers of the same or even higher purchase prices. This is because sellers are looking for the highest possible price, the lowest risk of the purchase contract failing to close, and the shortest time to close.

Good news: you will not need to keep your cash tied up in the property forever. After you purchase and improve a property, you have the option to refinance and pull out 75–80 percent of the cash you invested. This money can be used to replenish your savings account or to purchase another short-term rental property.

Refinancing Your Home or Securing a Home Equity Line of Credit

You may have more access to money than you realize. If you are a homeowner, you may have equity locked inside the walls of your primary residence. To access this equity and convert it into investable capital, contact your primary lender. Discuss with them the available equity and associated costs of a home equity line of credit (HELOC). A HELOC allows you to borrow from the existing equity in your home, usually at favorable rates.

An attractive benefit of a HELOC is that you can take only what you need. For example, if you have $100,000 in home equity, your loan will be set up as a line of credit that will be available to you when you need it to purchase your short-term rental property.

Interest is only paid on the amount that you withdraw. You can choose to use less than the full amount available to you, and you will not owe interest on what you do not withdraw. This provides flexibility as you consider different properties and the demands they will make on your budget. As your short-term rental property begins to generate cash flow, you can allocate a monthly amount to pay off both the interest on the HELOC and to pay down or pay off the associated line of credit.

First-Time Homebuyer

If you are a first-time homebuyer, the United States government has a loan-backing program known as a Federal Housing Administration (FHA) mortgage loan. If you have a credit score over 580 as well as a steady job, you may qualify for a loan with a purchase down payment as low as 3.5 percent under this program. Note: under FHA guidelines, you would be required to live in the property as your primary residence for one year.

If you or your spouse are active-duty or retired military members, you may qualify for a Veterans Affairs (VA) home loan with no down payment required. An FHA loan may be used to purchase a property with one to four units under one roof. More details on these loan programs can be found at hud.gov or FHAloans.com.

Second Home Loan

If you currently own your primary residence and are considering purchasing a vacation rental property, you are in a great position. Lenders typically think of home loans in three categories: Primary Residence, Second Home, and Investment Property. The bank will welcome you as a second homebuyer, as they are very familiar with this concept. I often say that your primary mortgage lender is waiting for the day you walk into the bank and say, "I am thinking about buying a house on the lake or cabin to enjoy with my family." Banks typically respond, "We've been waiting for you!"

Expect second home loans to have slightly higher interest rates, credit score requirements, a larger down payment, or higher closing costs. The good news is these loans are typically easy to obtain. To be eligible for a second home loan, the property must be 50 miles or more from your current residence, and you will need to certify that you plan to spend a minimum of fourteen nights there per year. As long as you spend fourteen nights at the property annually (or 10 percent of the time the property is rented to others), you are within IRS compliance to rent the space for the remaining dates.

If you anticipate investing in additional properties, now is the time to establish a relationship with a local mortgage broker. You will need to explain your financial situation and investment goals so he or she can help you plan the best ways to finance your growth. Ask your real estate agent for mortgage broker connections and meet with two or three brokers to find the best professional for your needs.

Loans Beyond a Second Home

Once you have received a primary and second home loan, lenders will regard any future acquisitions as investment properties. Some of my clients have dodged this lending barrier by applying for primary and secondary loans as an individual. Then their spouse applies for an additional primary and secondary home loan as an individual. Allow your moral compass to decide if this approach works for you.

An investment property loan will most likely entail higher interest rates, higher down payment requirements, and lower debt-to-income ratios when compared to a primary or secondary home loan. However, at this point you will also be generating additional cash flow from your initial investments. As you begin to consider an investment loan, it is important to conduct an in-depth search for the best available programs. I suggest reaching out to multiple mortgage brokers and real estate investors in your network. You are becoming a real estate investor and should start networking with other investors to access financing contacts whom they personally recommend.

Another avenue to explore is local credit bureaus in the area you have selected for investment. Local credit bureaus do not have the customer base or reach of national banks. Because of this, they are focused on making investments in their communities. If you are able to explain the value proposition of a short-term rental property, a local credit bureau may turn out to be a great loan source.

Asset-Based Lending

The short-term rental industry is a relatively new phenomenon. A short-term rental property is not a well-known investment, such as a second home or vacation home. Nor is it a multifamily apartment building. This means that financing specifically for short-term rental investments is not prevalent. However, the financial services industry is beginning to understand the opportunity of lending to short-term rental investors, so financing opportunities continue to evolve. Visio Financial is one example of this. Visio was created for the express purpose of serving the needs of short-term rental hosts. Investment One and KRAM Capital are two additional asset-based lending companies to consider.

There are some notable differences in how primary and secondary houses are evaluated by lenders versus how multifamily real estate properties are evaluated by lenders. Because multifamily real estate properties offer the closest approximation to short-term rental properties in terms of financing opportunities, it is crucial to understand these differences. A traditional home loan mortgage is based on the following factors that pertain to the mortgage candidate: personal credit history, earning stability, and the ratio of total monthly debt payment obligations to monthly income. In other words, the bank is financing you and making risk decisions based on the probability that you as an individual are ready, willing, and able to make your loan payments. By contrast, multifamily lenders are making risk decisions based on the following factors that pertain to the asset in question: the intended asset's cash flow and the underlying value of the asset. Lenders do not consider the loan applicant's personal financial factors in such situations.

Short-term rental properties are similar to multi-family assets based on their stable, growing monthly cash flow. I predict that more financial institutions will begin to offer products suited for this asset class with the goal of assisting efficient growth of short-term rental investors. Periodically conduct an internet search for short-term rental lenders. This will keep you apprised of any new asset-based financing companies and options.

Buy > Rehab > REPURPOSE > Rent > Refinance > Repeat

The BRRRR (pronounced "burrrr") methodology of real estate investing is an overarching system popularized by author and co-host of the *Bigger Pockets* podcast David Greene. This is a great construct for viewing your short-term rental portfolio growth. While this model is most commonly applied to long-hold properties, I added an additional "R" to the traditional BRRRR system to make it more applicable to short-term rental investing: Repurpose.

Buy—Starting with the Buy, or Buy Right, axiom, I use this first "B" to remind me to seize the opportunity at hand. This motivates me to make cash offers. A property deal cannot make you money unless you win that deal. As previously mentioned, cash offers are attractive to sellers and help win deals.

Rehab—Rehabbing a property entails executing a variety of potential steps, outlined in Chapter 6. Briefly, they include the following: low-, moderate-, or high-budget renovations; enticing decor; and High Dynamic Range (HDR) photography.

Repurpose—This is the additional "R" that I have added for short-term rental investment. Repurposing a property previously used as a single-family getaway home into a full-occupancy short-term rental is an ideal way to maximize your return on investment. List your rental on a popular online travel agency (OTA) such as Airbnb and keep rental occupancy as high as possible.

Rent—Revenue paid as rent by guests on Airbnb and other platforms is collected by the platform and deposited directly into the host's bank account at the time of guest check in. Unlike the long-term rental experience of nudging tenants for monthly rent checks, your cash flow is automated, and new funds are received every few days from new guests. As a short-term rental host, you also have the ability to raise or lower your prices between guests to achieve higher rental revenue or maximize your occupancy rate.

Refinance—It is wise to refinance your property after you have forced an increase in value (appreciation) by improving the property and establishing it as a cash-flowing asset that supports a higher valuation. This is called a cash out refinance, and you can choose to do this at any time if interest rates have improved or if you believe that the appraised value of your property has improved. If done correctly, you will be able to recapture the majority of money spent on improvements and on the original down payment for your property. Note that cash out refinance loan terms are frequently 75 percent loan to value, so, at worst, you will recover 75 percent of the new appraised property value. Given the variables of how long you wait to refinance, market appreciation, and your forced appreciation via repurposing and establishing a cash flow history, it is possible to regain significantly more than 75 percent of your initial investment.

Repeat—This "R" encourages you to take your recovered capital and reinvest in another short-term rental property. I like to grow my portfolio by two or three properties per year. This volume of growth allows me to follow the BRRRRR methodology with new properties while maintaining and managing my current properties.

Owner Financing

Is owner financing a myth or legend of yore? Owner financing is an agreement in which the buyer makes mortgage payments to the seller for an agreed rate and length of time in place of a mortgage payment to a bank. Owner financing does exist, but like many things in life and in real estate, hard work and persistence are necessary to find it.

The first step in procuring owner financing is to identify the type of seller most likely to be open to this idea. If the property you want to purchase is an income-producing asset for the owner, then owner financing may be a viable option. This type of financing is less likely to be attainable if the property you want to purchase is the owner's primary residence or weekend getaway.

Owner financing provides the property owner/potential seller a more secure revenue stream as compared to the revenue stream from renting or leasing the property. Why? Because year-to-year leasing incurs risks, such as non-payment of rent, troublesome tenants, repairs and maintenance, loss of income during tenant turnover, and the headache of continually sourcing new renters.

There are two forms of owner financing. One is specifically called "owner financing." In this scenario, the current owner can sell the property to you, while acting as the bank to generate monthly income. In this purchase format, the seller now has you as the buyer making the mortgage payment, which is a safer income stream than a monthly tenant lease payment. Additionally, they no longer have to maintain the property or find new tenants. The owner is further protected, like a bank, by holding a lean on the deed to the property. This is why owner financing situations can be attractive to sellers, especially older investors looking to prune their portfolios.

Owner financed properties are paid off and clear of mortgages. The seller takes a down payment and "finances" the rest of the amount to the buyer through a mortgage and a promissory note. At closing, the deed is immediately transferred to the new owner in his or her name, as would occur in a traditional sale. With owner financing, if the buyer were to default on the loan, the seller would have to go to an attorney and complete the traditional and expensive foreclosure process.

The second form of owner financing is called a contract for deed or an installment sales contract. The main difference between the two forms of financing is the way in which the deed is transferred. Contract for deed deals may have a very similar term structure to classic owner financing as described in the first scenario, but the deed is not transferred at the time of the sale. The deed is held in escrow until the contract is paid off. In this situation, if the buyer were to default on the loan, it is easier for the seller to take the property back and skip the foreclosure process. Do note that a contract for deed is not permissible in several states.

The ability to spread out capital gains taxes is another attractive factor for sellers when considering the contract for deed option. In this scenario, capital gains taxes are still paid by the seller, but the payments are spread out over the years of the contract with the buyer. For example, if a property owner sells a property under the traditional method for $70,000 more than he or she purchased it for, they would be required to pay taxes on that $70,000 gain immediately after the sale. In contrast, in a contract for deed purchasing scenario, the owner pays taxes on the down payment received at the time of purchase, and capital gains taxes on any additional profit from the sales price will be spread out over the term of the loan. This means that the owner will only pay taxes on the smaller portion of the gains, as they are allocated over each year.

A strong motivating factor for a property owner to offer owner financing to a buyer is the speed and cost at which the transaction can take place. The owner does not need to prepare the property for market if he or she has a ready buyer. Most importantly, the owner can avoid paying a real estate agent listing fee of 5-6 percent, thereby increasing their sale profit. Depending on the property value, this can be a significant motivating force for seasoned investors.

Do not overlook the advantages of speed, cost savings, and tax savings when proposing owner financing. Owner financing is a viable option for sellers who are seasoned investors but may be viewed as confusing or less legitimate than a traditional transaction to the typical homebuyer.

Partnership

The phrase "time is money," often attributed to Ben Franklin, is highly applicable to real estate investing and the raising of capital. Even if you currently lack funds for your first short-term rental investment, simply by having acquired knowledge from this book, having identified a target market and property, and being sincerely motivated to do the work, you possess valuable assets. As you begin to articulate your short-term rental investment acumen and the amount of capital needed to get started, you become attractive to potential investment partners.

The bigger challenge is finding the right partner and equitably dividing responsibilities. You can begin by listing the major responsibilities for each party:

- Finding the deal
- Finding the best mortgage lender and terms
- Funding the down payment and closing costs
- Funding improvements and furnishing
- Providing labor to prepare the property for listing
- Providing labor to operate and manage the listing, pricing, and guest communications
- Managing housekeepers and repair vendors

Realize every partnership situation is different. If you find a partner with whom there is mutual trust, responsibilities can be negotiated to achieve an amicable arrangement for both parties. Below is an example division of responsibilities one of my mentees used in a recent partnership.

Partner A has capital to invest, and Partner B has short-term rental experience, as well as time to devote to operations:

- Partner A will fund 100 percent of purchase price, improvements, and furnishings.
- Partner B will act as the managing partner, providing the deal opportunity, the labor to prepare the property for listing, and the labor to ultimately manage all aspects of operations.
- Partner A will be paid 75 percent of profits until half of the invested capital is repaid.
- Profits will be split 50/50 once half of the initial funding is paid back by Partner A.

Variations of this partnership can be created based on the specific contributions each partner brings to the table. It is important to note that at the onset of the agreement, the cash funding may make the deal happen; however, over time, once the cash is repaid, the time to manage and operate the investment becomes more valuable. This makes it important for each partner to agree on a timeline for exiting the partnership. Will this be a long-term endeavor? Will one partner have the opportunity to buy out the other? Will the partners agree to sell the property within a specified period of time? With good communication and a written agreement that addresses both short-term and long-term scenarios, partnerships can be very efficient vehicles for getting started in short-term rental investing.

Venture Capital

Venture capital is a way of raising funds to start a business by soliciting money from investors. One of my mentees used a "go big" venture capital strategy to scale his investment portfolio shortly after acquiring his first short-term rental property. Tony is an entrepreneur with a large network, so he decided to raise a capital fund to invest in short-term rental properties. Armed with the specific details on acquisition costs and investment returns from his first cabin, he developed an organized pitch deck and raised money from a small group of investors. Tony said it was the easiest money he has raised in his career.

In his own words, Tony decided to raise a small fund because he wanted to diversify his own purchasing across a larger portfolio. His fund bought eleven properties last year, and he is now raising Fund Number 2 in order to purchase another one hundred properties. Tony believes the short-term rental space can drive great returns, and he loves the idea of doing something on a large scale.

When asked about the drawbacks or cons of his funding approach, Tony noted that in order to obtain the same financial reward for himself, he needs to manage a lot more operations for his investors. That being said, there is significantly higher revenue potential once the fund amasses dozens or hundreds of properties. And Tony would not want to deploy the amount of capital needed for that number of properties from his own pocket.

Tony is not alone in his fundraising approach. Many successful short-term hosts who have experienced high returns are now pursuing a venture capital model. A prevalent sentiment among professional investors is that it is just a matter of time until established private equity and venture capital firms begin deploying capital into short-term rental portfolios in order to gain exposure to potential high rates of return. If this scenario occurs, it could offer a lucrative exit opportunity for hosts to sell their portfolios to investment firms at premium prices.

1031 Exchange

The 1031 exchange is another powerful strategy for investors who already possess an existing investment property, such as a long-term rental property. A 1031 exchange is named after the Internal Revenue Service (IRS) tax code 1031, which allows investors to defer taxes on the sale of an investment property, as long as they reinvest the sale proceeds into another equivalent investment property.

Consider this scenario: my mentee Dan owns a single-family home that he has been leasing out on a yearly basis, but now he wants to get started with a new short-term rental property. If Dan sells his existing property, he would be required to pay capital gain taxes on both the appreciation of the property value and the depreciation expenses he deducted for each year that he owned the property. Under the rules of a 1031 exchange, Dan can defer taxes by reinvesting the proceeds from the sale of his existing property into an investment property of equal or greater value.

As with any tax code, specific rules and restrictions apply. So before you sell any property, contact a qualified intermediary, which is an organization that specializes in 1031 exchanges. To find a qualified intermediary, ask your accountant, conduct a google search, or visit the1031investor.com to find recommendations and learn more.

Self-Directed Individual Retirement Account

The self-directed individual retirement account (IRA) is yet another investment strategy fueled by IRS tax codes. If you have been working for a number of years and contributing to an IRA, hopefully your account grew through both contributions and appreciation. Did you know that these funds can be used to make investments in real estate? Your current traditional IRA, Roth IRA, and in some cases your 401(K) retirement savings plans can be converted into a self-directed IRA.

As the name suggests, you have the ability to direct the investment vehicle for your savings. Real estate is a common application for self-directed IRAs. It is important to note that the same rules for traditional IRA contribution limits and withdrawal restrictions apply to self-directed IRAs. Specifically, you will not be able to draw profits from your short-term rental property, but rather the profits will remain in the retirement account until you reach the appropriate age to make withdrawals. Therefore, if your investment goal is building a large nest egg quickly, this option might be ideal for you. However, if you are seeking access to cash flow, then a self-directed IRA may not be your best approach.

If you are committed to getting started in real estate investing and your retirement plan is your only source of start-up capital, it may be worth deferring the cash flow into retirement savings to gain experience in short-term rental investing. Similar to the 1031 exchange, there are many rules and regulations governing this tax-exempt investment vehicle. It is wise to research self-directed IRA custodians and explore your real estate investment plans and goals with several of them.

High-Yield Non-Traditional Wildcard Investing

If the size of your current bank account and salary have you calculating a long wait for investment capital to accrue, consider investing in cryptocurrency. Small investments in crypto coins and associated support services have the potential to accelerate your savings plan through huge, overnight gains.

I systematically invest in Bitcoin, Ethereum, Dogecoin, and Coinbase to both build and diversify my asset investments. If you are new to crypto investing, all of these investment vehicles are available on Robinhood.com. Once you have a cash-flowing rental property, you can systematically pull a small portion of monthly profits and reinvest them in crypto. You will not miss a few hundred dollars per month, and the potential upside could be enough to fund your next short-term rental acquisition.

I employ a dollar cost averaging approach to crypto investing. Dollar cost averaging is the action of systematically investing equal amounts of money, at regular intervals, regardless of the current price of the asset. Select an amount you can comfortably live without. This could be $100 per month or $1,000 per month. As previously stated, the trick is to automate the investment on a preset schedule.

Conversely, if you have made substantial returns in prior crypto investments, you may wish to take some money off the table. Reinvesting crypto capital into a stable, cash-flowing asset like short-term rentals is a wise investment strategy.

Calculating Expected Returns

The One Percent Rule

Investors in buy-and-hold long-term rental properties use a metric known as the One Percent Rule. It is a quick litmus test to gauge a property's investability. Simply stated, if the expected top line rental lease payments exceed one percent of the purchase price, then the deal passes the One Percent Rule test. For example, if you are considering purchasing a rental property for $320,000 and the expected monthly rental income exceeds $3,200 per month or greater, then it passes the test. Most investment properties would have a hard time generating a 1 percent return, but that is why it is a quick, deal-determining tool.

Not many opportunities come along in buy-and-hold investments that pass the One Percent Rule examination. However, in short-term rental investing, you can manage a $320,000 property investment to easily yield over $3,200 per month. Short-term rentals hypothetically incur more expenses and a greater time commitment than long-hold rentals, but balancing out those additional operating costs means greater monthly income potential. With proper setup and management, short-term rental investors can expect two to five times higher returns than long-hold investors can expect. My properties and my mentees' properties routinely yield 3–5 percent monthly income compared to purchase price, making them outstanding investments.

Capitalization Rate = Net Operating Income / Current Market Value

The capitalization rate or "cap rate" is another commonly referenced ratio for expressing the investment value of cash flowing assets. A cap rate between 5 percent and 10 percent is considered a good investment. To use this index, you must first understand and calculate net operating income. Net operating income is what is left over after subtracting all operating expenses from the revenue generated by your property.

Continuing with our example: a property with a gross annual income of $96,000 with $48,000 subtracted in total operating expenses yields a net operating income of $48,000. Recalling the example property purchase price was $320,000, the cap rate looks like this:

$48,000 / $320,000 = 15 percent Capitalization Rate

Cash-on-Cash Returns

Cash-on-cash returns are a better metric for evaluating the use of your valuable and limited capital. This paradigm measures the total capital invested against the net annual income. Here is a model of the cash required to bring a $320,000 vacation rental property to market:

20 percent Down Payment*	$64,000
Closing Costs**	$10,960
Furnishing and Decor	$18,000
Total Cash Outlay	$92,960

*Assumes 20 percent down payment, although some may qualify for 10 percent down.

**Assumes closing cost of 3 percent of purchase price.

From our example property we have calculated annual pre-tax cash flow of $48,000 secured by investing $92,960.

$$\text{Cash-on-Cash Return} =$$
$$\text{Annual Pre-Tax Cash Flow / Total Cash Invested}$$

$$51.63 \text{ percent} = \$48,000 / \$92,960$$

This is an example of cash-on-cash return calculation. It is also closely based on a rental investment I recently made. The cash-on-cash model is an excellent tool for evaluating how best to deploy your capital against the opportunity to invest in other assets.

Where else can you find an investment that yields 50 percent return on your capital? The historic average return on the S&P 500 stock index is approximately 13 percent. Cash on cash returns clearly illustrate the power of short-term rental investments. If you can save a portion of your short-term returns, you will have the capital to repay your loan or to make a second investment in just over a year. If you continue the original savings plan you adopted when preparing to invest, you can accelerate this timeline. Alternatively, if you choose to procure more short-term rental properties, the timeline between your first and second purchases can be condensed significantly.

Average Daily Rate/Price Per Square Foot Investability Score

A quick metric I use when speaking with clients about viable investment markets is the ratio of average daily rate (ADR) to price per square foot (PPSF). Residential home prices are firmly rooted in market comparable sales, which are tied directly to price per square foot. As you evaluate a potential investment market, you can easily gather price per square foot data. Short term rental rates expressed as average daily rates can be obtained from AirDNA.

If properties similar to the one you are interested in purchasing are selling for $200 per square foot and the average daily rate in that area exceeds $200 per night, this indicates a good investment-buying environment. ADRs in established vacation rental markets routinely command nightly rates in the $200 to $300 per night range. However, if you are looking at a beachfront market, you can expect to see a price per square foot in excess of $400. While beach properties may be appealing, they often fail the ADR/PPSF analysis.

→ Chapter 5 Takeaways ←

- There are a multitude of traditional and non-traditional avenues to source money for a short-term rental investment.
- Use the BRRRRR model of real estate investing to quickly understand the steps of short-term rental investing. Repurposing your investment is key.
- Apply the One Percent Rule, Cap Rate, or Cash-on-Cash metric to calculate the investability of a property you are considering purchasing.

→ Further Reading ←

Creative Cash: The Complete Guide to Master Lease Options and Seller Financing for Investing in Real Estate by Bill Ham

Bitcoin and Cryptocurrency Trading for Beginners 2021 by Nicholas Scott

Cryptoassets: The Innovative Investor's Guide to Bitcoin and Beyond by Chris Burniske and Jack Tatar

→ Further Learning ←

Tune into the *BiggerPockets* podcast for more information and motivation around real estate investing.

6. DESIGN WITH YOUR GUESTS IN MIND

The majority of your listing views and bookings will be initiated by young to middle-aged women. Airbnb data indicates that 54 percent of bookings are made by women across the globe. In my market, 83 percent of individuals who engage with my listings are women. Give this demographic what they want: a clean, minimalistic, stylish interior with a nice kitchen and bathroom. The outside of your property can be rustic, but the inside must be beautiful. Women tend to do trip research, find a listing, consult with accompanying family or friends, and book the Airbnb. If you want maximum bookings, design with your guest demographics in mind.

What Not to Do

Avoid the "hodge-podgery approach" to decorating. We have all visited a getaway place that was a repository for kinds of mismatched furniture, quilts a great-aunt made, mugs from the back of six different cousins' cabinets, and the mounted deer head grandad shot back in 1965. This decor may create a sense of nostalgia for family and friends, but it will not work well for a short-term rental.

It is a good practice to avoid over-theming a space. We have all visited a relative or an Airbnb that went overboard with owls, apples, or antlers. Less is more when it comes to design. You can create a light overarching theme, but do not have bedspreads, curtains, lights, and towel bars with the same creature on them. That gets kitschy quickly, and kitschy is the opposite of clean and modern. Less is also more when it comes to scents. While you do not want your property to have an uncleanly odor, it is wise to avoid the use of candles and air fresheners with scents that may irritate your guests with a sensitive sense of smell.

Try to resist the temptation to make the place your own, even if you plan to spend time there. Do not decorate with personal photos; they make anyone who does not know your family feel uncomfortable during their stay. You should also avoid keeping family heirlooms and personal items in your rental. Think of how terrible you would feel if a guest accidentally ruined the cast iron skillet you inherited from your great-grandma. Instead, keep them in a lockout closet for when you and your family stay in your short-term rental.

What to Do

Create a beautiful space that will appeal to guests, withstand constant usage, and not break the bank. Give yourself grace. This is not your personal home, and no one will judge you as the designer. Most times you will never meet your guests. Peruse other Airbnb listings to get a sense of what you like and do not like. You can head to LurayCabinLife.com to look at the interior design of our listings.

Look for inspiration in a few home design catalogues such as *West Elm*, *Pottery Barn*, and *Crate & Barrel*. Clip looks you like and put them in a folder. Alternatively, take photos of them, and save them in a file on your phone. Spend some time on Pinterest making virtual pinboards of your favorite design ideas. You can search for modern farmhouse, boho chic, urban cabin, or whatever style appeals to you. Browse boutique hotel websites and print or pin any rooms that jump out at you. There is no end to the sources for inspiration!

If you have stayed in hotels with an element or piece of furniture you loved, try to incorporate it into your listing design. This allows you to capitalize on a concept that someone paid a top designer to create. It is completely okay to borrow and build upon ideas from professionals.

While it is important to find inspiration, do not feel compelled to recreate exactly what you have found. Every property is different. Start with your inspiration and allow the ideas and decor that best enhance your space to lead your design. Decorate how you like and with a color palette you like. Staying true to your own happy place of design makes it easier to shop and create a cohesive flow throughout your short-term rental. So, set your budget, pick your colors, begin painting, and start shopping! This is the fun part!

Less is More

Recall your best hotel and Airbnb stays. Such places tend to have lovely decor but also have plenty of space for your suitcases and personal items. As a host, you want to provide a beautiful space with plenty of space. Resist the temptation to keep adding design details. Culin refuses to stay anywhere with fussy toile or floral embellishments, and he is not alone in this sentiment. Your listing should not be spartan, but it also should not be brimming with knickknacks. Less is more.

Lisa

We loved staying in this hidden cabin in the woods. The rustic environment, combined with the modern, elegant but simple decor, was a perfect combination for a romantic getaway. The hosts' attention to little details -- from the well-equipped kitchen to a swinging chair on the screened-in porch, made it extra special. This is a real gem!

Color Palette Selection

Instead of buying a few pieces you like at several stores and trying to make them work together, try selecting a color palette as your first step. Creating a cohesive color palette will help you as you decorate your short-term rental. Choose one bold color and one to two neutral colors to work with. If you are unsure how to get started or what might look best, paint companies post their most popular color combinations on their websites, on Pinterest or Instagram, or in printed brochures at a variety of store locations. Look around and find the combination that best suits your space and your overall vision.

In rentals, it is strategic to use your chosen bold color for an accent wall and some of your furniture. These touches of color create focal points that will pop in photos and grab the attention of browsers. One of my design signatures is a blue velvet couch. I love how opulent they look, how comfortable they are, and how they contrast against wood tones and lighter colors.

Once you have your accent color and/or furniture, paint your other walls a neutral color. Reference your palette when adding art, pillows, dishware, and rugs. Your goal is to create a cohesive, clean look in each room. Create a space that anyone would want to spend time in.

I am a huge fan of bright, white ceilings, trim, and curtains. White ceilings and trim make rooms look bigger and brighter, while white curtains lend a more upscale hotel feel to the space. While I love white paint, I avoid white and light-colored furniture. Such pieces may look lovely in photos, but they will be ruined after one spilled cup of coffee or one melted chocolate bar.

The Yellow Door Effect

Chapter 13 has a story about Danielle painting a cabin blue and the front door yellow. This birthed a new mindset for us. We like to tell our mentees about the Yellow Door Effect. It essentially means: turn off your residential home mindset and associated limitations.

Give yourself the freedom as a host to experiment with bright paint colors, add uncommon amenities, and implement any other ideas you have to make your listing one of a kind.

I just encouraged you to be creative, but there are a few caveats. There is a fine line between interesting and weird. Make certain that whatever changes you implement will be attractive to the majority of guests, not to a minority. Also ensure that your changes are functional. If you add an amenity that is fragile, future guests will be upset if they find it damaged for their stay.

Short-Term Rental Shopping Mindset, Best Practices, and Sources

Purchase quality design items, but do not get attached to them. Over time, things will break, snag, or be lost by guests. Consider buying duplicates of "perfect" items, such as duvet covers, canvas art, or rugs so that you can easily replace them. Remember, you are not decorating your dream home, you are designing a space that is comfortable for your use, as well as for guests.

Showstopper Light Fixtures

Replacing dated, builder-grade light fixtures with something visually interesting is a great way to update and upgrade your short-term rental. Light fixtures seldom get broken, so you can afford to purchase designer-style fixtures.

Push yourself out of your design comfort zone when it comes to light fixtures. Remember, you do not live there, and guests are looking for eye-catching listings. If you have a modern rental, go for a sputnik-style chandelier. If you have a modern farmhouse, find a wood and black metal hanging fixture with Edison light bulbs. This is the place to go big. The more light in your space, the larger it will look in photos and in person.

Culin and I spent several hours installing a showstopping black metal chandelier over the dining room table in a log cabin. The fixture was so heavy that we had to pile boxes under for support as he wired it into the ceiling. He mused that it was a waste of time and money. That same day, we interviewed housekeepers, and every single one of them oohed and ahhed over the fixture. Years later, we still have guests message us to ask where we purchased the chandelier. This and other experiences have taught us that show-stopper fixtures matter in a short-term rental.

I find the majority of my overhead lighting on Wayfair.com and Overstock.com. You can search by style, number of lights, and finish material. The Hampton Bay Boswell Quarter Lighting Collection at Home Depot offers several fixtures to emulate or purchase. IKEA is a great resource for standing lamps and table lamps, but their overhead lighting can be very challenging to install. Whatever lighting you choose, using Edison light bulbs adds additional visual interest and a coolness factor to your short-term rental.

Pro Host Tip: Purchase open-cage light fixtures whenever possible. Their lack of glass makes them less likely to break, less likely to trap dead bugs, and makes it easier to replace light bulbs.

Linens

Hosting has changed dramatically in the past few years. Old-school hosts used to require guests to bring their own linens. That line of thinking will not result in 5-star reviews in today's day and age. We are hosting in the time of luxury Airbnbs. Our customers have 5-star hotel expectations, and making up beds with their own sheets is neither luxurious nor fun.

It is a best practice as a host to purchase all of your linens and towels in the same color. The two most popular colors for sheets and towels are white and gray. By selecting one color and one brand, you enable your housekeeper to wash all linens together, which saves a considerable amount of time. He or she can also use pillowcases from any sheet set when making beds, which is also a timesaver during a turnover.

The water quality in your short-term rental may dictate the linen color choice for you. If you have purchased a property with a well or in a rural community, test the water by washing an inexpensive white towel. If you have high iron deposits, your water may stain your white towel yellow. In this situation, consider gray towels and bed linens instead of white.

We purchase all of our sheets, towels, light blankets, and bathmats from AmazonBasics. AmazonBasics is Amazon's private label brand, which is typically high quality and offers reliable and identical replacements at lower prices than other companies. The benefit of purchasing from AmazonBasics, aside from price, is how easy it is to replace towels. You can purchase a set of six bath towels, hand towels, and washcloths. Then, if a washcloth is stained or torn, you can purchase replacement washcloths without having to purchase an entire set. You can do the same thing with their sheet sets.

Purchase at least two sets of bed linens for each bed or pull-out mattress and at least two sets of towels per guest to accommodate your maximum number of guests. So, if your cottage sleeps four guests, buy eight sets of towels. Duplicate purchasing allows your housekeeper the ability to immediately swap all linens in the event of a late checkout. In a worst-case scenario, he or she can take the dirty linens to a laundry mat to be ready for the next turnover.

We advise keeping duplicate linens in a cleaning closet with a digital lock. This ensures your emergency linens are available during a worst-case scenario. Should guests need extra towels or a set of sheets for the pull-out couch, you will be able to share the digital lock code with them. This closet is also where all cleaning supplies and bulk paper products should be stored.

If you live near a body of water, buy separate towels for guests to use outdoors. We stock our cabins with striped beach towels from AmazonBasics. This helps prevent guests from using your nice bathroom linens at the river, beach, or lake.

Pro Host Tip: When your sheet sets arrive from Amazon, use a Sharpie to mark the tags of each set with the corresponding bed size (i.e. K, Q F, or T). Again, this saves your housekeeper time and stress. Instead of wasting time figuring out which fitted sheet goes on which bed, he or she can look at the corner tag and have more time to make the rest of your rental sparkling clean for the next guests.

Duvets and Blankets

Purchasing duvet covers and separate inserts is an excellent idea as a host. The covers can be quickly washed and dried instead of dealing with a bulky, one-piece duvet or comforter. Buy at least two duvets and inserts for each bed so your housekeeper can make a quick turnover.

I tend to buy duvet covers with pintucking because they never look wrinkled coming out of the dryer. The Caloundra Microfiber Reversible Modern & Contemporary Duvet Cover Set from Wayfair is a great example and one of my design go-tos. Reasonably priced duvet inserts can also be found at IKEA, Amazon, or Target.

In the theme of simplicity, duvet covers should not be heavily patterned. Select solid colors that will contrast with your wall colors in photos. The exception to this are duvet covers in children's rooms. I have done a modern pattern that makes the room more inviting. The key is to find duvet covers that appeal to children and teens alike. You do not want a baby room; you are striving to design a fun room.

Cozy, solid-color throw blankets are a great purchase. I always have a basket of throw blankets next to the couches in our rentals. It makes a cabin feel much more like a home and adds the Danish concept of hygge. I typically source throw blankets in luxurious fabrics from HomeGoods, Tuesday Morning, or Marshalls.

Curtains and Blinds

When outfitting a new short-term rental, I always buy white curtain panels on Amazon. The panels I favor are $16 per panel and are made of polyester. They photograph beautifully and can be cleaned in the washing machine or with a Tide pen. I have successfully rinsed red wine out of one of these panels using only water. They are miraculous design items that lend an air of hotel chic to your space. Again, it is wise to buy two extra panels for quick replacement during turnovers.

Room-darkening blinds or shades are a wonderful addition to any bedroom. We purchase them at Lowe's and always install them in children's rooms. Anyone who has or travels with children recognizes the value of a dark room. On our first vacation with our son, he woke up with the sun shining in his window at 5:00 a.m. It was such an opposite-of-vacation experience that we tacked up black garbage bags in his room that evening. Bless your guests with rooms where their children can easily fall asleep and stay asleep. Room-darkening shades can also be selected as an amenity on your Airbnb listing.

Short-Term Rental Art

Art in a short-term rental can go wrong quickly. Avoid hanging art just to fill a blank wall. I recently stayed at an Airbnb for a friend's birthday. The space was beautiful, but there were fifteen or more random pictures and paintings, featuring fruit, horses, birds, and various outdoor scenes. There was no overarching theme, color, or style. The hodgepodge art detracted from the space and sparked many "Why would someone do that?!" conversations. The house would have been better if there had been no art on the walls.

Avoid abstract, 1980s hotel art, as well as photos of your family, taxidermied animals, or any art involving people. Ideally, you want to find art that is somewhat contemporary, in your color palette, and that makes sense in your space and overall design.

Art does not have to be limited to paintings. Metal wall art, oversized clocks, driftwood, mirrors, and canvas maps are all excellent ways to decorate walls. For our rustic cabins, I have found sliced geodes and crystals mounted on linen in shadow box frames. Their natural beauty works with the log walls, and their modern framing makes them stand out visually.

Art does not have to be expensive. Especially when a wall calls for a large piece, I search Etsy for printable art. For example, I type "printable abstract watercolor blue" into the search box. Hundreds of listings for printable art pop up. When I find the perfect art to fit a space, I pay $5 to $20 for the download, and then I send the file to Staples to have it printed in the size I want. Next, I pick up a frame at Michaels or on Amazon. And presto! Gorgeous, large-format art for under $40. If you want to skip Staples and save time searching for a frame, you can use a service like FrameBridge.com to print, frame, and ship your print to your rental.

Once I select a piece from a particular artist, I make sure to look at other prints from this artist to see if there are other works I can incorporate into the design I am creating. This is an easy way to achieve continuity of style throughout your space. In our first cabin, I have three framed abstract watercolors of mountains. I also selected the same artist's rendering of birch trees for the master bedroom. Aside from Etsy, HomeGoods and IKEA are alternate places to look for reasonably priced art.

Furniture

Buy new furniture in the same metal or wood color whenever possible. It's totally fine to repaint a bookshelf or mix in an accent chair from Facebook Marketplace, but too much mixing and matching gets messy.

Think about function, future guest use, and durability along with furniture design. Furry rugs and seats look great initially but will become matted with use. Rugs that must be dry cleaned add additional expense and turnover time for your housekeeper. Metal or well-made wood bedframes are great choices that look nice and last for years. Sofas with a pull-out mattress make your listing more appealing to larger groups and can generate extra guest fees. Fragile or poorly made furniture will result in headaches and guest complaints. I source the majority of our couches, bedframes, and dining room sets from Bob's Discount Furniture, Value City Furniture, At Home, or WayFair. They have good prices and good quality for short-term rental furniture. Smaller furnishings such as accent chairs, desks, benches, and coffee tables can be found on Wayfair or at HomeGoods, Marshalls, World Market, or IKEA.

If at all possible, purchase a king size bed for your short-term rental. It is a sought-after amenity on Airbnb. There is a percentage of the population that need a king size bed due to their physical size. For many other people, a king-size bed is a luxury and something they love to experience on vacation. Adding a grand bed or two is one more way to differentiate your short-term rental and increase its booking and revenue potential.

Pro Host Tip: If your short-term rental will have a king-size bed, or beds, add the words "king bed" to your Airbnb listing title if at all possible. This will catch the attention of any guests who are searching with a king-size bed as a filter, as well as those who may not filter for bed size but still appreciate this particular amenity.

Mattresses are a key item for guest satisfaction. Invest in a mattress that will appeal to the masses, not just your personal preference. Head to a mattress store and talk to a salesperson about their most popular mattress, or poll your friend group for a favorite. Whatever mattress you end up purchasing, be sure to protect it with a mattress encasement. We purchase zippered mattress protectors on Amazon and know that our mattresses will be protected from any spilled liquids, dust mites, allergens, and bed bugs.

Pro Host Tip: Do not purchase a memory foam style mattress for a top bunk. They are very heavy, and this makes changing the sheets incredibly difficult.

Adding a desk or leaning shelf desk to your listing gives your guests a space to answer a few emails or do homework over the weekend. With work-away trips on the rise, desks are becoming critical pieces of furniture in short-term rentals. If you do not have space for a desk, look for bureaus that have a pull-out desktop or for fold-flat desks that can be affixed to a wall.

Dishes

It is difficult to beat the price, style, and durability of stoneware from IKEA. We have their DINERA line of plates, bowls, and serving dishes in all of our cabins. We are not the only hosts who see the value of IKEA dishes. We have encountered them in almost every Airbnb we have rented, from Spain to Prague to Greece. I always buy matching stoneware coffee cups, silverware, and various kitchen utensils from IKEA. It is advisable to purchase an extra set of dishes and coffee cups to use as replacements.

Wine glasses are a must-have for your kitchen. Consider purchasing stemless glasses, as they are less likely to be knocked over and broken. I purchase stemless wine glasses in 20-packs from Amazon. Ten glasses are placed in a kitchen cabinet and ten are left in the cleaning closet for when our housekeeper needs to replace one.

Kitchen Amenities

Kitchen appliances are an inexpensive and excellent way to wow your guests. In many cases, guests who do not cook regularly at home will use vacation time to make a big breakfast or family meal. Think about the appliances you use the most in your kitchen, and make sure to stock your listing with the same. I always purchase a Keurig combination carafe and pod coffee maker, microwave, toaster, griddle, waffle maker, crock pot, blender, mini-food processor, and hand mixer for our properties. If you anticipate hosting European guests, an electric kettle is also a necessity. While you do not want cluttered cabinets, making sure you have more than the basics for guests to cook with will result in 5-star reviews. We always outfit our short-term rental kitchens with a full set of pots and pans, mixing bowls, baking sheets, cupcake tins, a cheese board, serving platters, a knife block, a garlic press, a wine key, a can opener, measuring cups, and measuring spoons. Aside from these items we also provide ground coffee, sugar, flour, and an array of spices and cooking oils. Our goal is for any guest to start cooking and be delighted with what they have, not frustrated by what is missing.

> **Pro Host Tip:** If your short-term rental accommodates six or more guests, purchase a four-slot toaster. We had guests suggest this in private feedback, and it makes sense. If you're making breakfast for six or eight people, the time wasted waiting for a two-slot toaster is annoying. We now have four-slot toasters in all of our larger cabins, and guests are very happy.

Bathroom Amenities

Providing toiletry items, a quality hairdryer, and a few items to pamper your guests is essential as you outfit the bathrooms in your short-term rental. Mini hotel-style shampoos, conditioners, and soaps can be sourced on Amazon. I prefer luxury minis, while Culin opts for more economical options. Our compromise is to launch our new listings with luxury minis and then order more standard replacements as they are consumed by guests. Other hosts opt to use wall-mounted soap and shampoo dispensers, which have the benefit of cost savings and lower environmental impact.

Be sure each of your bathrooms are outfitted with frequently replaced shower liners, cushy bathmats, full-length mirrors, a hairdryer, and extra toilet-paper rolls. If you are short on vanity space, purchasing a hairdryer bag gives you the option to hang it from a wall hook. We also provide makeup mirrors, bath salts, and individually wrapped mini makeup removers to ensure our guests' delight at our properties.

Area-Specific Amenities

Providing amenities that allow your guests to enjoy your listing's surroundings is a great way to increase satisfaction and elicit rave reviews. Things like hard- and soft-sided coolers and a basket of sand toys make the beach more fun. Fishing poles, kayaks, and picnic baskets are wonderful amenities for lake or river rentals. Binoculars, bird books, and local trail maps make a wilderness getaway that much more special for guests.

Providing amenities also ensures that guests do not have to stop vacationing to go purchase an item, and it protects their vacation budget. No one wants to pay $50 for a cooler when they have one back at home.

AMENITIES
CHECK OFF THE SURPRISE AND DELIGHT AMENITIES
YOU HAVE AND CIRCLE ONES TO CONSIDER ADDING

Keurig combination coffee and k-cup pot	Desk/office space
Coffee & creamers	Pool/Beach/Lake towels
Complimentary bottle of wine	Throw blankets for couches
Pack n Play crib	Fishing poles/archery set
Spices and olive oil	Corn hole/horse shoes
Griddle	Outdoor twinkle lights
Waffle Iron	Robes
Muffin/baking tins/cookie sheets	Children's books and toys
Crock pot	Q-tips, cotton balls, face wipes
Hanging Basket Chair	Dog treats

Airbnb Design Hacks:

- Use see-through furniture as much as possible. They make rooms look bigger and more interesting.
- Add hanging basket chairs or egg chairs inside.
- Add a wall-mount shelf desk for work-away trips and for online school.
- Use plenty of faux plants throughout the space. They provide contrasting color and visual interest
- Make a child/teen-friendly bedroom.
- Make inviting outdoor spaces with chairs, hammocks, a grill, benches, fire pits and hardscaping.
- Juxtaposition is a designer's friend. If you have rustic log walls, use a soft fabric like a velvet couch or throw pillows for contrast. If you have a modern space, consider adding faux plants hanging on the wall to bring a natural texture.
- Play with textures and fabrics to create a more upscale look. You can do this by adding pillows to beds and couches. Incorporate a sheepskin or leather accent chair.

Safety Items

There are a few safety items that hosts should have on hand for guest emergencies. Be sure to purchase a first aid kit, fire extinguisher, smoke detector, and carbon monoxide detector. These items not only help keep your guests safe, they may also protect your short-term rental property.

Micro Amenities

Adding micro amenities to your listing is a great way to increase guest interest before they book and to guarantee their satisfaction during their stay. A micro amenity is anything under $350 that you can add to the interior or exterior of your short-term rental for guests to enjoy.

One of the best micro amenities to include in a property is a hanging basket chair placed either on the front porch or in a bedroom. Guests love hanging chairs! Remember, they are looking for things they do not have in their residence. Danielle once booked an Airbnb in Prague simply because it had a hanging basket chair on the rooftop.

Any micro amenity that makes your outdoor space inviting is a win with guests. Building a fire pit with local stones or pavers from Home Depot is a fantastic and budget-friendly amenity. If you do not have enough yard space for a fire pit, consider adding a small fire table to your deck. We have hung swings under decks for children to use, replaced decrepit outdoor furniture with luxe modern rockers, supplied fishing poles, constructed archery areas, provided corn hole games, and hung twinkle lights from porch rafters. Simply adding a nice gas grill or hanging a hammock is a micro amenity that guests will enjoy.

Living room micro amenities include a nice TV, a DVD collection or smart TV to stream movies, battery-operated candles, and a basket of cozy blankets. Depending on the size of the room, another amenity to consider is a foosball table. Providing indoor entertainment items, such as games, puzzles, and Legos, is an inexpensive way to keep guests happy during poor weather or cancelled activities.

Child Amenities

Little guests are just as important as adults. If they are not happy, no one is! Micro amenities to include for children are a pack-n-play, a baby gate, children's plates and utensils, a basket of stuffed animals, toys, a puppet theater, bean bags, and a collection of children's books and DVDs. You might also consider adding an outdoor playhouse, treehouse, sandbox, miniature picnic table, or a swing hung from a tree branch.

One of our favorite child amenities is a teepee. Danielle decorated a room with a lighted teepee in one of our first cabins, and we were overwhelmed by how much guests enjoyed it. Child amenities will differentiate your listing and frequently will be the thing that has guests paying more to secure a place their children will love.

Pet Amenities

Another thing to consider is a pet-friendly rental. This is a huge amenity for many guests. If you're going to the mountains, the beach, the river, or the woods, you typically want to bring your dogs. If a short-term rental does not allow pets, it means guests must pay for them to be kenneled somewhere.

If you want to welcome pets, you should make sure your floors are not carpeted and that you add amenities for pets. I highly recommend a flooring product called CoreTek. It looks like wood or tile but is virtually indestructible. I have installed it in three of my cabins so far with zero pet damage. The key takeaway as you begin to decorate is this: if you want maximum occupancy, you must cater to your renters' needs and tastes, including their pets.

If you have a pet-friendly property, do not overlook furry friend amenities. Many guests love their pets as much as their children. Consider leaving a canister of dog treats as a surprise and delight item. Create an outdoor area or amenity for dogs. List any local dog parks and dog-friendly wineries, breweries, and coffee shops in a framed sign or in your house manual. Anything you can add as a host that makes your listing more appealing to pet owners is a great investment.

Surprise and Delight

Guests love to be surprised by hosts with small treats. These surprise and delight items could be a bottle of wine, a mini jar of local honey, bath salts, or a s'mores kit for the fire pit. Your first five reviews are particularly important when you launch your listing. Showering your guests with treats helps guarantee rave reviews.

It is important to select items that are shelf-stable, available for bulk purchase, and easy for your housekeeper to set out. Surprise and delight items that are a bottleneck for your housekeeper will not last long.

It is also wise to keep surprise and delight items out of your Airbnb listing. This way, they are a surprise, and if for some reason the treat is not set out, your guest is not disappointed. Imagine if you booked a place that promised freshly baked cookies, and when you arrived, there were no cookies. You would be disappointed! But if you never knew to expect cookies, you would be none the wiser.

After testing many items, we have streamlined our surprise and delight item to flavored creamers, biscotti, and a bottle of red wine. A custom label invites guests to relax and enjoy cabin life. When we lived in Greece, Danielle and I loved finding a bottle of wine in Airbnbs we booked throughout Europe. It made us feel welcomed, and a glass smoothed any tensions from whatever traffic or travel complication we experienced before our arrival.

Create a House Manual

Another way to ensure guest happiness is to create a house manual. This manual functions as a paper concierge. Think of what information you want to be given when you stay somewhere new. Things like the wi-fi network name and password, where certain light switches are, and instructions for turning on the sauna are examples of what should go into your manual. We fill a leather, three-ring binder with specific cabin tips, amenity instructions, restaurant recommendations, area attractions, brochures, and restaurant take-out menus. Flip to Appendix 1 to find an example of our cabin manual.

A house manual does not just benefit guests. By providing important information, a manual dramatically reduces the number of questions a guest will ask you as a host. It also benefits your listing ratings. Guests who can immediately find an answer to a question instead of messaging a host and waiting to hear back have a better overall experience and therefore leave a better review on Airbnb.

Shannon
The place was. It's the perfect mix of modern decor with the cabin aesthetic. My only regret was not booking a longer trip. The little notes left around the house from the owners were helpful.

Install a Keyless Lock

Keyless locks are beneficial for both hosts and guests. They allow guests to check in at any time without someone needing to meet them with a key. Guests do not have to wait for a host or helper to check them in, and, as a host, you do not have to wait around for late guests.

By replacing the front door lock to your short-term rental with a keyless lock, you also negate the possibility of guests losing the key or locking themselves out of your rental. Before we had keyless locks, we often received calls from guests who took their dogs for a walk or went stargazing and locked themselves out. That is a terrible scenario to deal with at midnight.

Keyless locks also make it easy for you to give housekeepers, handymen, and contractors access to your short-term rental without needing to be present or make copies of a key. Depending on the type of lock you purchase, you can issue each guest a new access code, as well as track when the door was opened and shut. These features add an extra layer of security for your short-term rental. We cover this topic in detail in Chapter 10.

Live in Your Listing for Several Days

As eager as you may be to list your property on Airbnb and start generating revenue, it is imperative that you spend three to five days staying at your property. Actually living at your listing will help in myriad ways.

First, you will meet your neighbors and hopefully forge friendships and trade phone numbers. Strive to be the host that everyone in the community loves. It is better to receive a phone call from a neighbor about noise at your short-term rental than to receive a message from guests that the police came by.

Living in a place allows you to learn its quirks. You learn which light switch turns on the back deck lights, how long it takes the hot water to flow in the shower, and where to locate the source of the inevitable weird sound.

If we had not lived in one of our cabins, we would not have discovered the resident whippoorwill in the woods nearby. These little brown birds scream "whip-poor-will" at the top of their lungs on evenings during mating season. Being able to assure guests that they are having an amazing encounter with nature—not a monster—has been very helpful. Also make sure all that wonderful wildlife stays outside your rental. There's nothing worse than arriving to a house full of ants or mice. Be prepared to hire a pest exterminator or set rodent traps or place pet-friendly poisons (i.e., diatomaceous earth) out of sight—such as in the basement or crawlspace.

Finally, living in your rental will help you fill any hospitality gaps. You will realize that you need a bottle opener, coffee filters, laundry basket, scissors, or any other necessary day-to-day amenities. Our guests are impressed by how comfortable they feel in our cabins. Why? Because they have everything they need to simply enjoy their time away.

Professional Photos and the Importance of HDR

Anyone in real estate knows the value of professional photos. The same is true for your short-term rental. Spending $200–$300 on professional photos will make your listing jump out to individuals searching on Airbnb. Most Airbnb listing photos are taken with an iPhone. Your photos will look better, attract more guest views, generate more bookings, and all of this will feed into the

Airbnb algorithm. Your \$200–\$300 investment in professional photos should easily result in \$15,000 in rental revenue. Make the investment and schedule a session with a professional photographer!

High Dynamic Range (HDR) photography is a technique commonly used in professional real estate photography. Multiple images of different exposures are blended together to create a superior final image. For example, a photographer may take three images, one underexposed (too dark), one overexposed (too bright), and one with a generally balanced exposure. Those images are then blended together, using the middle image as a base, and taking the light areas from the underexposed image and the dark areas from the overexposed image. This brings out much more detail than a single image could and makes the final image closer to what the eye would see if you were standing in the room.

There is another more advanced version of HDR called flambient, which we use on all of our short-term rental properties. This technique introduces flash photography as well as multiple exposures, and generally involves more detailed image blending during post-processing. Flambient photography allows a photographer to achieve even more accurate colors and lighting than standard HDR photography. These photos visually jump out of your computer screen, making a listing both compelling and memorable.

What Home Photographers Wish You Knew

I asked our long-time photographer, Carson, what he wished hosts knew before having him shoot photos. His advice is spot on.

Owners should ensure that the home is clean and staged as they would like it to appear in photos well before the scheduled photo shoot. This seems obvious, but homes are ill-prepared much more often than you might think.

If you are unsure if your short-term rental is photo ready, go through each room and stand in every corner. If you can see anything out of place, dirty, or undesirable from that spot, it needs to be fixed before the photographer arrives. Remember, if you can see it, the camera usually can too.

Take time to look out through each of your windows. Frequently, a room looks great, but owners miss something unsightly in view of the windows, such as a riding lawn mower or garbage cans. Remove outdoor eyesores whenever possible. It is terrible to have a gorgeous shot of a master bedroom ruined by a pile of scrap wood visible through the window.

Photographers typically take their best home photographs alone. This does not mean you should never meet your photographer or discuss shots you would like, but the more people in the home, the more difficult it is to shoot.

Be thoughtful about lighting and time of day when scheduling a photo shoot. Good natural light on the front of the house can make or break a stunning first impression. Similarly, if the back of the house or a side patio is more impressive during certain hours, factor that into your shoot time. Do not delay your photos for a particular season. Instead, consider booking a secondary mini shoot to capture beautiful leaf colors, spring blooms, or how your property looks with a blanket of fresh snow.

How to Find the Right Photographer

Curious how to find a professional photographer for your new short-term rental? It can be as easy as a Google search for "real estate photographer" followed by your town or city. Check out a few of the photographer websites that appear from your search. Scroll through those photographers' galleries and reviews. If you like what you see, reach out for a quote.

Another way to find a real estate photographer is to ask a local real estate agent. They typically have a go-to company or individual for photography. Some real estate photography companies will only work with real estate agents. If you are not an agent, pay your real estate agent to hire the photographer for you.

We met Carson when we paid our real estate agent to hire him to shoot our first cabin. Carson's skills are amazing. It was like Christmas Day when I received our listing photos from him. Carson started McRae Visual Media LLC, and we now recommend his company to all of our clients in Virginia.

Pro Host Tip: Create a Style Guide for Your Housekeeper. Once you have your fabulous property photos, you can utilize them for more than your Airbnb listing. I create style sheets with photos of how each room should look for our housekeepers. Guests move candles, blankets, chairs, and sometimes couches to other rooms. Providing a visual template for your housekeepers helps them know what goes where. This ensures that your guests will always walk into the home design they booked on Airbnb.

People Will Rent Imperfect Properties

It is easy to get overwhelmed by the number of things that need to be changed, renovated, and purchased to make your short-term rental perfect. Perfect is the enemy of done. Take a deep breath and remember that people will happily rent imperfect properties.

Our second investment cabin had a terrible kitchen. The washing machine was next to the sink, the cabinets were all mismatched, and there was a shelf built over the washing machine for the toaster. There were also three types of carpet throughout the space. When we started renting out that cabin, investing in a new kitchen and floors simply was not in the budget.

What did we put on the market? A cabin with a rustic exterior and a clean interior. Our paint was fresh, our furniture new, throw rugs covered most of the tragic carpet, and the old tool shed was turned into a garden pub. We took photos of the kitchen and floors so guests knew exactly what they were renting.

Seven months later we blocked off a week of the rental calendar to renovate the kitchen and replace the carpet with laminate flooring. It looked like a totally different place! After these renovations, we took new photos and were able to increase our rates, which increased the cabin's revenue by more than $1,500 per month.

→ Chapter 6 Takeaways ←

- Design with your guests in mind. Incorporate macro and micro amenities into a streamlined decor plan that will appeal to women.
- Invest in surprise and delight items for your guests, but do not add them to your listing.
- Live in your space for a few days before listing it to catch any missing necessities.
- Invest in professional flambient HDR photography to make your listing pop on Airbnb.

7. CRAFTING YOUR LISTING

Selecting Your Platform

It is best business practice to list your short-term rental property on a single platform. This is known as sole sourcing. You may choose Airbnb, VRBO, or Bookings if you live outside the United States. Airbnb is the platform that I prefer. Sole sourcing removes the headache of keeping track of multiple calendars across multiple platforms while reaping rewards for your listing by maximizing a single platform's algorithm.

I realize the decision to commit to a sole platform may seem counterintuitive. You may be thinking, "As a host, if I can list my property ten different places for free, shouldn't I do that? It's free marketing and broader exposure. Shouldn't I be on all those platforms?" The answer is no. Why? Because Airbnb is a search engine for spaces, much like Google is a search engine for websites and information. By listing your rental on multiple platforms, you are diluting your search engine optimization. This results in low-rank placement across multiple platforms. The lower your rank, the fewer people will see your listing.

Let's use an example to illustrate this concept. If my short-term rental property is 100 percent booked for a given month with 50 percent of my bookings through Airbnb and 50 percent of my bookings through VRBO, does either platform consider my listing as fully booked? No. Is my listing making all the money it can for Airbnb? No. And their platform algorithm knows that. The Airbnb algorithm rewards listings high-occupancy rates by placing them higher within search results, which means more guests view your listing.

If you are diluting your listing across two platforms, neither algorithm is going to reward you. Most people do not understand this and consistently do the wrong thing. I coach all my mentees to focus on making one platform's algorithm really happy. This approach helps their listing rise to the top of search results and generate the most bookings and highest revenue possible.

Have you heard the expression that you can't sell the same house twice? You certainly cannot book the same night at your short-term rental twice! Listing platforms are economic animals. Airbnb ultimately wants guests to find and book accommodations as quickly as possible to generate service fees from the host and the guest. They are constantly changing their algorithm to drive revenue and booking ease.

Airbnb is also at war with the other booking platforms for market dominance. So, as a business, they want to reward you as a host for bringing in revenue for their company. In addition to financial motivation, Airbnb does not want to lose any percentage of their market presence. They want to reward you for being their sole partner. This keeps your listing and its revenue stream on their platform.

There are also demographic differences between the two main booking platforms. VRBO is an older company that was acquired by HomeAway's parent company Expedia Group. Both VRBO and HomeAway traditionally cater to full-week destination bookings. Their users also skew to a slightly older age bracket. Airbnb is the newest booking platform, and while bookings can be a full week, shorter stays tend to be the norm.

As we mentioned in Chapter 1, Airbnb users are typically younger individuals who are looking for experiences and interesting stays instead of hotel accommodations. According to an article written by Jaleesa Bustamante for iPropertyManagement.com, 64 percent of Airbnb guests are under the age of 44[17]. As a host, I witnessed firsthand Airbnb's rise in prominence. When our nanny mentioned that she and all of her friends were asking for Airbnb gift cards for Christmas, I realized how much the culture of travel had changed. Her comment helped me understand that Airbnb is vital to the travel industry and will continue to be so in the future.

If you are currently fully booked on VRBO, I am not saying to remove your listing from their platform. However, if you are succeeding on VRBO, do not add your listing to Airbnb. To optimize your success, you have to commit to one platform. Both platforms are viable, and 95 percent of the strategies presented in this book will apply equally to either platform.

If you are a new short-term rental host, I recommend listing with Airbnb. The company's size, exponential growth, and the host of third-party software tools created to plug into their platform will make your journey to success faster and easier.

Listing Setup

After you successfully purchase your short-term rental property, you can begin setting up your Airbnb listing. This can be a confusing process, so use my step-by-step list. You can learn about the details and best practices for each step in the Listing Setup Deep Dive which follows.

10 Step Overview

Step 1: Sign up as an Airbnb host

Step 2: Create a new listing

Step 3: Set nightly pricing

Step 4: Create your title and listing description

Step 5: Upload your photos and descriptions

Step 6: Review your listing and be certain your rental and you as a host are guest-ready

---

17 https://ipropertymanagement.com/research/airbnb-statistics

Step 7: Publish your listing and manually adjust your calendar pricing rates

Step 8: Create your PriceLabs account and connect it to your listing

Step 9: Complete your listing

Step 10: Automate your messaging

Listing Setup Deep Dive

▶ Step 1: Sign Up as an Airbnb Host

It is important to note that you can get started on your Airbnb listing before you are actually ready to go live. Beginning the process will allow you to slowly fill in the blanks for your listing and will prompt you to start thinking about the best ways to describe your rental to potential guests.

Creating your host account with Airbnb is very straightforward. If you would like my guidance with setting up your listing, use my ambassador link at: www.airbnb.com/r/culint to set up your account. If you choose, this will permit me to access and review your listing with you before it goes live.

When setting up your host account, be sure to use the email and phone number at which you want to receive all communications from the Airbnb platform. You will want to download the Airbnb app if you do not currently have it on your smartphone. The app will send you notifications about guest bookings, messages, cancellations, and more. It gives you a convenient pulse point for your listing and communication with your guests. This is it! You are at the cusp of your journey as a short-term rental host!

▶ Step 2: Create a New Listing

Now that you have created a host account with Airbnb, you can create your first listing. Select the type of rental you have and add your rental address. Then select the number of guests you can accommodate. If your rental has a pull-out couch or futon, be sure to factor these into your guest number. Next, select your space's amenities from the list provided.

The amenity list on Airbnb ranges from central air conditioning to board games to outdoor dining areas. It is a great source for amenity ideas to include in your space and descriptions. This list is constantly updated, so check back every few months to see if there are more things you can share as amenities.

▶ Step 3: Set Nightly Pricing

Once your listing is created, you have the ability to set nightly pricing. Airbnb will suggest a price range based on other rentals in your area. Select a quick interim nightly price, knowing that it will soon be overwritten by the PriceLabs tool after you publish your listing. I will cover the PriceLabs tool in Step 9 of this chapter and in greater detail in Chapter 8.

Do not opt into Airbnb Smart Pricing. This is not a third-party dynamic pricing tool, and most hosts find that it sets pricing below a nightly rate with which they are comfortable. Also, be sure to uncheck the box agreeing to discount your first three guest stays.

▶ Step 4: Create your Title and Listing Description

Put thought into your listing title. Titles are what potential guests see when looking at Airbnbs in your area. The title should be something descriptive and memorable that mentions key amenities, such as a king bed, hot tub, sauna, water access, or views. This is not a real estate MLS listing, so titles like 3BR/1B/900SF will not be easily remembered when potential guests discuss and compare where they should stay.

Here are examples of our listing titles:

Listing name

Modern Mountaintop Retreat 💜 **Screened Porch**
Getaway bliss, river rock shower & more!

Shenandoah Gem ~ Sauna ~ Walk to River ~ King Bed
Come enjoy the majest of the Shenandoah Valley - Watch th...

Blue Moon Log Cabin 💜 **Hot Tub and Walk to River**
Rustic cabin with modern luxury decor

Shenandoah Sunsets ~ Breathtaking Views
*Weekends fill fast, but we have great weekday rates!...

Shenandoah Hideaway 💜 **Garden Pub & Hot Tub**
Cozy, pet-friendly getaway with outdoor fire pit

Cedar River Retreat ~ River Access ~ Hot Tub ~ King...
Gorgeous log cabin nestled in the forst with lovely river...

When writing your listing description, use the five hundred-word maximum to your best advantage. Sell on the "experience" of your place. Describe what it feels like to be there, the great things about the space, the amenities, local attractions, etc. Bullet points are a great way to convey a large list of amenities or attractions.

You can also peruse other listings in your area to get a sense of what you do and do not want your description to be. If you are not exactly sure what to write, put a few ideas in this section for starters. You can always return to this section and update your description before you activate your listing.

Here are two examples of our cabin listing descriptions:

Breathtaking mountain top cabin with private river access • 180 degree sunset views from 4 decks • Minutes from downtown Luray & Massanutten Resort • Backs to 400 acres of private woodlands • Fully equipped & stocked kitchen • Gas Fireplace • Grill • Onsite washer & dryer • Queen sofa bed • Foosball table • Satellite internet • Smart TVs • Paved driveway • Extensive DVD collection + games • Come feel the amazing mountain top breezes.

Come enjoy the majesty of the Shenandoah Valley - Watch the sun set in a hanging basket chair on the porch, melt away your stress in the sauna, or simply enjoy relaxing by the floor to ceiling gas fireplace. Create lasting memories by hosting a family game night with our 8 person game table. This newly built cabin is walking distance to the Shenandoah River and Shenandoah River Outfitters Canoe Company. Shenandoah National Park, Skyline Drive, and Luray Caverns are all within a 20-minute drive.

Pro Host Tip: Make the most of the *About the Space* section of your listing description. Write a paragraph about how it feels to live in the space and then detail the best aspects of your short-term rental. Many hosts miss this opportunity to share more tantalizing details about their property outside of the five-hundred-character limit of the listing description.

▶ Step 5: Upload Your Photos and Descriptions

This is where a $200–$300 investment in professional photography will earn you thousands of dollars each month. The first five photos are what guests will see in your listing preview, so make them count. Use your best exterior photo, a gorgeous shot of an interior space, a photo of any amenities (ie, sauna, hot tub, or fire pit), a photo of the master bedroom and a photo of the kitchen or bathroom. These are the images guests most want to see.

Next, fill in additional photos that show all of the rooms of the rental as well as outdoor spaces and local attractions. These photos help guests answer their internal booking questions, such as the following: What does this place look like outside? What do the bedrooms look like? Are the kitchen and bathroom functional? What cool things can I do if I book here?

Be honest with your photos. If your bathroom is so-so, show it with the shower curtain open. Guests do not mind imperfect places, but they hate feeling duped by misleading photos. As you select and upload your photos, create thoughtful captions by clicking the pencil icon in the top right corner of the photo. Use creative captions to help guests picture themselves in your rental. Which caption would you find more compelling as a guest? "Master bedroom" vs. "Drift off to sleep in the master king bed with luxury linens and breathtaking river views."

As with your photos, it is also important to be honest in your listing description. If your location is truly minutes to an attraction, be sure to include that fact. But do not stretch the truth about your location. Do not say something is within walking distance if it is not. Best practice is to list the distance in miles to attractions. This allows guests to come to their own conclusions about your location and not feel cheated in any way.

▶ Step 6: Review Your Listing—Be Certain Your Rental and You as a Host Are Guest-Ready

Review your listing, paying attention to grammar, authenticity, and a logical flow of photos. Make sure your rental is ready and that you as a host are completely ready for guests before you publish your listing. Is your rental clean, with all amenities assembled and in place? Is your housekeeper ready to do guest turnovers?

I tell my mentees to make sure that they are in front of their computer, at home or in their office, and to go to the bathroom before they publish their listing. Why? Because when you activate your listing, you are in no way finished. You are only halfway through the Airbnb onboarding process. There is at least an hour of critical work ahead of you. Several essential tools must be connected to your listing, and there are myriad internal Airbnb settings to adjust immediately in order to ensure the success of your short-term rental.

Airbnb says there is a twenty-four-hour lag before guests can view your listing. In my experience, listings go live immediately or within a few hours of being published. My mentee Phillip received his first booking while still on the phone with me as we were implementing post-publishing tools and changes. Fortunately, he was ready for guests to arrive the morning after his listing went live. Make sure you are in the position to wow your first guests, not scramble to get your place ready before they check in.

▶ Step 7: Publish Your Listing and Manually Adjust Your Calendar Pricing Rates

It is critical to manually overwrite your Airbnb calendar pricing as soon you click the *Publish* button. Go to the *Calendar* tab within your account and highlight all available days in the current month by dragging your cursor over the dates. Then click the *X* next to the *Smart Pricing* option, showing in the right column of your computer screen. This turns off the base rate suggestions from Airbnb. Type in a new high interim nightly rate of $300–$400 per night and click *Save* to have that price applied to all highlighted days in that month.

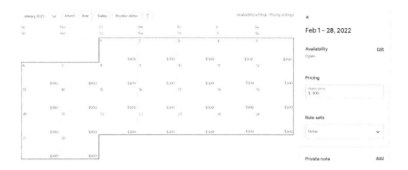

Image from Pricelabs Pricing Overview

www.pricelabs.co

Scroll down to the next month and highlight all days in that month as well. Follow the same process of turning off *Smart Pricing* and adding in your new interim nightly rate. Repeat this for the next twelve months in your calendar. For example, if you are publishing your listing in January 2022, fill in the monthly pricing through January 2023.

Inputting your new interim high pricing across your calendar will both give you breathing room to set up and connect PriceLabs and will protect you from guests booking several weeks in your calendar for very low rates. You do not want someone to scoop your place for Thanksgiving or Christmas at $89 per night while you are in the setup process. This has unfortunately happened to me in the past.

You have now manually overwritten the *Smart Pricing* suggested by Airbnb. It is wise to turn off *Smart Pricing* completely so it does not interfere with other tools you will plug in. Go to the *Menu* tab; select *Listing* from the drop-down menu; click *Pricing*, and click *Availability*. Then click *Edit* to the right of the pricing block and slide the toggle for *Smart Pricing* to the off position. You will need to confirm that you are turning off *Smart Pricing* and select your reason, which you will do in a pop up that appears.

While you are in the pricing section of your host account, you should turn off the *Suggested Monthly Discount.* One reason to do this is at $350 a night, it is not feasible for a guest to book your rental for an entire month at $10,500. They will ask for a discount. The second reason to avoid bookings over 28 days in length is that your role as a short-term host legally shifts to landlord. This makes evicting month-plus guests very difficult. Skip the lower rates and drama associated with long-term stays by sticking to your original pricing and short-term stays.

Note that Airbnb automatically blocks the first week on your rental calendar. This is something you must manually unblock. If you as a host and your property are completely ready for guests, highlight the entire seven days that are blocked, click *Available*, and enter your interim nightly rate.

►Step 8: Create Your PriceLabs Account and Connect It to Your Listing

As an overview, you will create a PriceLabs account and connect it to your new listing. Then you will experiment with base prices and review suggested prices. When you are comfortable with the base rate, you will do some manual discounting to attract those first few guest stays. Finally, you will sync PriceLabs with your Airbnb listing calendar, which will overwrite the high interim prices you initially set up.

PriceLabs is an extremely helpful and powerful tool that dynamically sets pricing based on real-time and historic Airbnb rental data in your market. It takes into account historically booked prices, other competitors' listing occupancies, and current search volume for available booking dates in your area.

For example, you may not know that there is an upcoming festival in your market on a particular weekend. While PriceLabs may not know about the festival either, it knows that searches in the area are up 80 percent that weekend, and it will increase your nightly rates for high-demand dates. On one occasion, a family booked my cabin for over $800 per night, comprising two weekdays and two weekend nights. I had no idea why the nightly rate was so high. Upon further research, I found out that there was a college graduation that weekend in a neighboring town. PriceLabs made me an extra $400 per night for that four-night stay.

Other third-party dynamic pricing tools, such as WheelHouse and Beyond Pricing exist as options. But PriceLabs is the tool I use and recommend to my clients. To set up your PriceLabs account, close your Airbnb tab as you will be prompted to do so during the account validation process. Next, go to pricelabs.co and create a login. Then click *Add Your Listing.* You will need to confirm your Airbnb login and enter a PriceLabs verification code that will be sent to your cell phone.

When your screen refreshes, click the green *Review Prices* button under the *Calendar* section. This allows the PriceLabs software to sync calendars with your Airbnb account, pull all pricing information, and make nightly pricing suggestions. You may be surprised by the variations you see. Take note of the suggested pricing for the month of December, presented below.

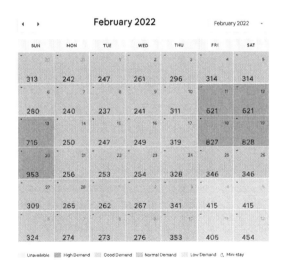

The next step is to click *Help Choose a Base Price* on the left side of your screen. PriceLabs will show you a suggested median price based on rentals in your market with a number of bedrooms equivalent to yours. This number is a suggestion that is typically a little high when first launching your short-term rental. You are not in live mode yet, so I suggest plugging in an experimental rate just below the median area rate and then clicking *Confirm*.

Review the nightly price suggestions that result from your experimental rate. How do you feel about them? Are they too low or too high? There is an art and science to setting pricing. Click on the first day of the month and highlight through the last day of the month to get an instant overview. This will calculate the average nightly rate and total revenue for that month. Make sure to review these numbers for several months.

If you are getting started in a low season, you may be surprised by how different your price suggestions will be later in the higher season. Rental rates are often higher in spring and summer months, as more people travel during those seasons. Test the intelligence of the PriceLabs algorithm. Look at the nightly rates for holidays, such as Fourth of July or Christmas. Open a peak month in your market, such as July for a riverfront property. Your nightly rates for those dates should be much higher than the base price you entered.

Your goal is to find a base rate with which you are comfortable and to allow PriceLabs to adjust nightly pricing according to its calculations of your market's supply and demand. Once you are happy with your base rate and overall PriceLabs pricing structure, toggle the *Sync Prices* button to on, and then click the gold *Sync Now* button. Next, open your Airbnb listing in a web browser. All pricing from PriceLabs should appear in your Airbnb calendar immediately.

If you are feeling overwhelmed by the concept and implementation of dynamic pricing, head to pricelabs.co. Their website offers numerous demonstration videos explaining how their tool works, best practices, and how to set up your account.

PriceLabs has endless customization options for hosts. I have covered the most important ones in this chapter for your initial launch. If you would like to learn more about these features and how to best optimize your listing, you can go to www.hostcoach.co to schedule a coaching consultation with us. Applying the level of technology offered by PriceLabs to your pricing is one of the main ways to reap maximum profits from your short-term rental property. It is a total game changer.

▶ Step 9: Complete Your Listing

Once your pricing is established through PriceLabs and synced with your Airbnb calendar, it is important to complete your listing. Airbnb splits the setup process into two phases: before going live, and after going live. The most likely reason for this is to reduce the friction of creating and publishing a new listing. However, this split creates a bit of a disconnect. You just published your listing, but there are now many live settings that need to be addressed immediately.

One key to Airbnb success is to have *Instant Booking* turned on. Airbnb wants their booking process to be similar to a hotel experience, where potential guests can be in their pajamas and book our place at 11:00 at night, instantly. Guests and Airbnb do not want the friction of having to message and wait for a host response before being able to book.

Set up *Instant Booking* by going to the Airbnb *Menu* tab. Select *Listing* from the drop-down menu and click *Pricing*. To the right of your listing name, you should see the words *Listed*, *Instant Booking*, and *Preview Listing*. If you see *Instant Booking* set to off, click on it, and on the next screen, click the button to turn *Instant Booking* on. Next, click *Save*. You now have *Instant Booking* activated, so guests can instantly book your rental the same way they would book a hotel online.

After turning on *Instant Booking*, you have the option to add three *Instant Book* requirements by clicking on the toggles next to each of them. The requirements you select must be met in order for a guest to use *Instant Bookings* to reserve your space. The first option requires guests to upload a government-issued ID to the Airbnb platform. The second option requires at least one recommendation from another Airbnb host and to have no negative reviews. The third option requires guests to read and respond to a message prior to confirming their reservation.

Many hosts view these *Instant Book* requirements as a way to safeguard their properties. As with many Airbnb settings, requirements are a personal choice. Hosts must balance guest vetting against the friction guests experience during the booking process. The only requirement I set for my properties is that guests upload a government-issued ID.

While you are on the page for *Instant Booking,* you can also set your cancellation policy. Click on *Cancellation Policy* to view the options; click on the one that is best for your rental; and then click *Save.* Cancellation policies are a personal decision as a host. All of my short-term rentals have the moderate cancellation policy selected. This allows guests to cancel five days before their check-in date and receive a full refund. The policy also gives me as a host five days to rebook those cancelled dates in my calendar.

It is also important to set a security deposit under the *Policies and Rules* section of your listing. Click *Edit Security Deposit* and enter the deposit amount. We set our deposit amount to be equal to an average night's stay at the property. Guests will not see or be charged this security deposit. But in the event of property damage, you as the host will be able to request reimbursement through Airbnb.

Set Minimum Night Requirements

Many new hosts like the idea of requiring seven-night bookings. Typically, this is because they want to make sure their calendars are full. In my experience, a seven-night requirement is an outdated practice that scares off individuals with less vacation time or smaller budgets. All of my short-term rental properties have two-night minimum stays. This actually keeps my calendar fuller than longer minimum-night stays. It allows guests with both longer stay and shorter stay needs to find and book my properties.

As you compete with other listings in your area with traditional seven-night minimums, your lower minimum night will make you attractive to visitors needing a shorter stay, and you will command higher nightly rates.

Set Cleaning and Extra Guest Fees

To set up your cleaning fee, go to *Listings*, *Pricing* and *Availability*, *Additional Charges*, and then click *Edit*. You can then type in your cleaning fee and click *Save*. Are you unsure what to charge your guests?

Cleaning fees are another personal choice for hosts. I charge my guests a cleaning fee, but I do not charge them 100 percent of what I pay my housekeeper. For example, if I pay my housekeeper $60 for a cleaning job, I charge my guests $40, which is approximately two thirds of the total.

My thought process behind this ratio is that guests are more comfortable with a slightly higher premium nightly rate that has a portion of the cleaning fee baked in than with a high cleaning fee. We have all experienced this, right? You are all set to book a property, and when you see the total, there is an extra $200 tacked on. This definitely makes me feel less excited about the booking and may scare off guests.

In the *Fees* section of your account, you can elect to set extra guest fees. Extra guest fees are an excellent way to increase your overall revenue. For example, you can charge $200 per night for the first three guests staying at your property and charge an additional $20 per night for each additional guest. One extra guest fee does not seem like much, but when six people book a four-night stay, that generates an extra $60 per night, for a total of $240 in extra revenue.

To implement your extra guest fees, click *Edit* and enter the amount you would like to charge per guest over your minimum number of guests. You will also need to indicate at what number this fee is applied. In my example, I would enter $20 per guest over three guests.

Many new hosts are curious about how to enforce their extra guest fees. My suggestion is to not worry too much about it. People are generally honest. You will waste time and stress yourself out trying to count guests on outdoor surveillance video. What you can do is a preemptive monthly audit. Look at the upcoming bookings for the next thirty days and see if any list only one guest. Occasionally, someone is doing a solo retreat, but most of the time, they missed where to add their number of guests. Send them a quick message asking if they are planning to stay by themselves. Usually you will get a response such as, "Oh my goodness, I totally forgot to add my three friends to the booking!" They then update their Airbnb reservation immediately.

▶ Step 10: Automate Your Messaging

The final step in your listing launch is creating responses for guest inquiries, bookings, check-in, and check-out. There is a great tool called Hospitable (formerly known as Smartbnb) that can help automate your messaging as a host. Chapter 9 includes an in-depth explanation of the tool, as well as samples of my messages.

Strategic Timing

If your property has a particularly high season (beach house people, I am talking to you!), try to strategically time when you publish your listing. I recently coached a couple who purchased a beach condo in South Carolina this fall, and I suggested that they complete all of their renovations this winter with the goal of being ready to list right before Spring Break, instead of rushing to list in late fall. Why? Because they are timing their listing to debut right as demand in their area is high. This will ensure that they maximize their new listing boost from Airbnb and secure bookings, great reviews, and Superhost status, which will then carry them through the slower beach seasons of fall and winter.

→ Chapter 7 Takeaways ←

- Selecting a single listing platform avoids calendar headaches and allows you to reap maximum algorithmic rewards for your short-term rental.
- Be sure your space and housekeeper are ready for guests to arrive before you publish your listing.
- Connect PriceLabs to your listing the moment you publish to avoid bookings at extremely low prices.
- After publishing your listing, be sure to activate and adjust several tools and settings to optimize your listing.

→ Tools & Technologies ←

PriceLabs is a powerful tool that can dynamically set nightly pricing for your rental based on real-time and historic Airbnb rental data in your market.

→ Further Reading ←

The Airbnb Story by Leigh Gallagher

8. SEARCH RANK PLACEMENT, CONVERSION OPTIMIZATION, AND PRICING FOR OCCUPANCY

Understanding how Airbnb works as a business and, specifically, what its algorithm measures are vital keys to your success as a host. It is important to understand that Airbnb is a search engine, also known as a search algorithm, just like Google. You can list your property for free, but the Airbnb search algorithm decides which listings are shown in what order for every user search. You will be competing for search placement against hundreds of other listings, and your goal is to be shown on the first page of search results in your market.

Ask yourself how often you look past the first page of Google search results. When you conduct an internet search for a piece of information, a service, or a consumer good, how many pages do you scroll through? Do you go past the first page? Maybe, but probably not. When you are looking for a rental property on Airbnb or VRBO, do you go past the first page? Maybe. But, again, probably not. This is why it is essential to know how to position your listing on the first page of search results for your area. Fortunately, I have some suggestions on how to do this.

To position your listing on the first page, you need to understand Airbnb's goals as a business. Airbnb has two primary goals: guest satisfaction and revenue maximization. While these goals are often aligned, they are also sometimes at odds with each other. Keeping these goals in mind, think about what Airbnb is going to want to see when deciding where to place your property on their platform.

Search Rank Placement

Search rank placement is the position in which your listing appears to viewers on the Airbnb platform. Consider how a potential guest thinks as they begin searching Airbnb for a place to stay.

This future potential guest most likely has in mind a destination, travel dates, and the number of guests in their party. What they do not know are the following two factors that influence their decision: the cost per night for properties in this area and the quality of accommodations available in this area. These are the questions the Airbnb algorithm is trying to solve when a visitor clicks the search button.

Copyright Ten:Eleven Press

Airbnb wants to show search results that future potential guests will find compelling and consequently will quickly book. This is how their company makes money and provides a great user experience. Guests are delighted to have found a great place quickly, at a great price, with great reviews. The Airbnb website and app make this process seem easy, but it is actually quite complicated.

Unlike Google, Airbnb cannot show the same top twenty search results each time, because their unbooked inventory is constantly changing. What if that amazing house with spectacular views is not available for the weekend you are looking to travel? What if, in addition to your basic search criteria, you also want to bring your pet or would like a hot tub? What if you need four bedrooms, a pack-n-play, and a cancellation policy that allows for a last-minute cancellation? What if you require an Instant Booking policy that will let you book and check in later today? Multilayered and multifaceted searches such as these continuously challenge the hardworking Airbnb algorithm.

Welcome to the Show

Consider the scenario of a future potential guest beginning their search after your new Airbnb listing is published. As a host, you have selected a property in a desirable location, decorated it well, outfitted it with every amenity, and taken professional photos. You have also written a compelling title and description, while pricing your space competitively within the market. This is your big moment as a host, and Airbnb wants you to succeed. Airbnb knows that as a new listing, you do not have any reviews or any wish list additions. Because of this they are going to give you a boost by placing you near the top of the search results for the next few weeks. Now is your time to shine, as you are evaluated by the traveling guest pool. This is also the time for Airbnb's algorithm to start building its own impressions of your listing—specifically your listing's ability to quickly convert views to bookings.

Views

First, some great news: for the Airbnb algorithm to reward you, viewers do not even have to book your property for the Airbnb algorithm to reward you. All they have to do is view it. Airbnb will measure and reward your listing simply because it has been seen more than other properties in those first few weeks. This is because Airbnb values the viewer engagement with their platform that comes with clicking and browsing through your listing.

Viewers may see your pricing and choose not to book, but you are still scoring points. The views are moving the ball in the Airbnb algorithm to elevate your listing rank, which means your property is shown more times. The more often your listing is viewed, the more likely you are to land that $800 a night booking two months from now. In addition to tracking views, the Airbnb algorithm also tracks clicks and wish list additions.

Click-Through Rates

Your listing will be evaluated on a metric called "click-through rate." A listing's click-through rate is the number of people who click on the listing from the search results in which the listing appears. The higher the percentage of clicks and views received, the better your listing will perform in future searches with similar criteria. By calculating the click-through rate, Airbnb is beginning to gauge how well your listing title and photos draw guests to engage further with your listing. This metric is then reported back to you by Airbnb as an average search-to-listing conversion.

Listing Engagement

Next, Airbnb will begin measuring the amount of time a viewer spends perusing your listing details. Are these viewers taking time to click through your photos? Are they spending time reading your listing descriptions? Or are they quickly passing over your listing and moving on to another potential place to stay? Longer engagement time with your listing correlates with higher search rank placements in the future.

≣ **Booking conversion**

| All listings | Sep 15 → Oct 15 | Rooms and beds | Regions | Amenities |

| 0.32% | 51.0% | 21.80% | 1.49% |
| Average overall conversion rate | First-page search impression rate | Average search-to-listing conversion | Average listing-to-booking conversion |

Conversion to Booking

Airbnb is dedicated to helping guests make a quick decision to book accommodations on their platform. This is where some of your policy selections can improve your search rank. If you have enabled Instant Booking with as few restrictions as possible, this will decrease friction in the guest booking process. Conversely, if you require guests to contact you for your evaluation and approval of their request to book, this introduces friction into the process, and the guest may elect to find a listing that is easier to book. If you have a strict cancellation policy, guests may be turned off by this inflexibility and may search for other listings. Also, if your nightly prices are out of range compared to other listings or if your listing lacks compelling amenities, potential guests will be inclined to continue shopping.

Circle of Rank

Your listing must receive views to get bookings. However, you also must have bookings to get more views. To generate more views, you need to earn higher placement in the search rank. To be placed higher in search rank, your listing must be viewed more. This is a mutually reinforcing cycle that can be leveraged to propel your listing to the top.

Therefore, another primary factor related to Airbnb rank placement is booking occupancy. Airbnb rewards listings that have high click-through rates, number of views, and booking conversions. The algorithm rewards listings with 90 percent or greater occupancy; this is a top-valued metric. If you achieve this metric, Airbnb is going to reward you by showing your listing above any other listing with lower occupancy levels. Conversely, listings with lower occupancy levels will be pushed below your listing.

The algorithm learns which listings can convert browsers into paying, satisfied guests. This means that if you have a great listing with professional photos and guest interactions that result in bookings, you will have a successful Airbnb listing. Airbnb will receive 3 percent from you as a host, along with an additional 12 percent from guests who book your rental property. They want to reward successful listing partners by placing them at the top of search results, so that you book more nights and they net more profits. It is easy to see how this quickly becomes an upward trend to success or a downward spiral toward disappointment. This important concept is overlooked by most hosts.

Guest Satisfaction

Your first guest booking marks the beginning of your evaluation by guests. This is your time to shine through excellent communication and hospitality. Your guests will be forming opinions of you and your property from the moment they book until the moment they check out. Upon checkout, Airbnb will prompt the guest to review their experience with your listing and with you as a host.

Airbnb prompts guests to evaluate their stay via a three-pronged approach: a questionnaire, ratings on specific criteria with seven main subcomponents, and an overall star rating. While the review questions are constantly changing, the overall star rating, specific criteria ratings, and all public and private comments are reported back to you as host. You are striving to achieve only 5-star reviews and glowing testimonials.

The seven subcategories for guest evaluation are as follows: accuracy, cleanliness, check-in, communication, location, value, and amenities. These categories are explained in detail in Chapter 12.

Pro Host Tip: If you have not booked and stayed in an Airbnb, do so. This will allow you to experience the rental process, from check-in to host interactions to the review process from the perspective of guests.

Reviews make or break your success on Airbnb. After your fifth guest review, Airbnb will begin to show your overall rating score, which it calculates by averaging the scores of those reviews. Five 5-star reviews will give you an average score of 5.0, while one

4-star review during these first five reviews will lower your overall score to 4.8. Likewise, two 4-star reviews will lower your overall rating to 4.6. Make sure to do everything possible to generate 5-star reviews as your listing launches.

Guests rely on your review score, as well as the public written reviews when making booking decisions. A high-average score and glowing reviews will amplify your bookings, while a lower score and lackluster comments in reviews will most likely scare potential guests away. Equally important, the Airbnb algorithm takes into account both the number and quality of your reviews when deciding where to present your listing in terms of ranked placement in future search results.

Copyright Ten:Eleven Press

3-Star Listing

Unimaginative title
Poor photos taken with a phone
No photo descriptions
Static pricing
All weekends booked for three months
3- and 4-star reviews
Slow host response time
Instant booking not available
Host must meet guests at check in
Strict cancellation policy

Copyright Ten:Eleven Press

5-Star Listing

Memorable descriptive title
Professional HDR Photos
Complete photo descriptions
Dynamic pricing
Full weekday occupancy
5-star reviews
Immediate automated messages
Instant booking available
Contactless check in
Moderate cancellation policy

Pricing for Occupancy

After approximately two weeks, the search placement boost that Airbnb's algorithm applies to new listings will wane. You are now competing unaided against all other listings in your market. So how do we win this competition while also maximizing revenues? The answer is pricing for occupancy. In essence, this means keeping your calendar full—but not too full too soon! Your property is only making you and Airbnb money while it is booked. It cannot generate revenue when it is vacant.

When pricing your listing, you must trust this maxim: only the market knows what your property is worth on any given night of the year. Most hosts adopt static pricing and maintain a set daily rate that does not change. This results in undercharging for most weekends and overcharging on weekdays. And this is exactly where 95 percent of hosts go wrong. Static pricing results in low to moderate occupancy rates, which translates into lower search placement and fewer views on Airbnb. It is a common host mistake to set a price of $250 per night based on what they believe their listing is "worth." In reality, what is your listing worth? It is worth whatever someone is willing to pay for it on any given night.

The price a guest is willing to pay to stay in your property will vary by the value that guest perceives your property to be worth in a specific date range. For example, if you create a unique listing with amenities that guests appreciate, then the value of your property for a holiday weekend, anniversary, birthday, or other special event will increase accordingly. When we were attending a friend's wedding at a winery, we paid a much higher nightly rate than we normally would be comfortable with. Why? Proximity to the winery allowed us to walk home from the ceremony and reception.

Assuming you have done everything correctly in setting up your listing, earning 5-star guest satisfaction reviews, and implementing dynamic pricing, what's next? Recall the instruction during initial listing set up to establish dynamic pricing around a guess about your optimal base rate. It is now time to circle back and adjust that base rate. The dynamic pricing tool uses its algorithms, which are based on supply and demand, to adjust your nightly prices up or down from the starting point of your original base rate. So how do you know if you have selected the correct base rate? And how do you know when to increase that base rate? The market will tell you the answers over time as you observe your occupancy rates.

Modifying Nightly Rates Based on Occupancy

Your goal as a host is to achieve 90–100 percent occupancy at the end of each month. However, if on any given day you are already 100 percent booked for the next 90 days, you will not have any inventory to sell. This means you have most likely underpriced your offering. Think of it this way: you have the power to take any listing to either 0 percent occupancy through high pricing or 100 percent occupancy through low pricing. The goal of setting pricing is to maximize the revenue from your investment. To achieve this, you can rely on data from PriceLabs. Ideally, you want to be no more than 50 percent occupied thirty days out and no more than 25 percent occupied sixty days out.

Because you can only rent your property to one set of guests at a time, it is a limited resource. If your property is booking rapidly, the market is indicating that your listing is in high demand. Where we have low supply and high demand, basic economics shows us that the price can be raised. A 50 percent occupancy rate thirty days out is a good benchmark for finding pricing equilibrium.

Copyright Ten:Eleven Press

Your thirty-day and sixty-day occupancy rates should inform your base price adjustments. If after a month on the market, your thirty-day occupancy rate is above 50 percent and your sixty-day occupancy rate is above 25 percent, you can feel comfortable increasing the base rate through your dynamic pricing tool. I suggest making small, incremental changes of $10 per night to your base rate once per month. Conversely, if after a month or more on the market, your thirty-day occupancy rate is below 50 percent, you need to either manually discount in the short term or lower your base rate. The longer your listing is on Airbnb and the more 5-star reviews you garner, the more price authority your listing will wield. Price authority is the ability to charge a higher rate than others in your market.

Anticipate a ramp-up period to reach your maximum rates. Over time, you will keep your short-term rental booked, so it will receive more views, and more people will save or wish list your listing, which will in turn increase the popularity of your listing. Guests will leave great reviews, which will make more guests interested in booking your place. Guests will also want to rebook your place, and the increased demand will drive up your nightly rate. My short-term rentals continue to increase in base rate year after year, and so will yours.

Near-Term Occupancy

It is critical to monitor your near-term occupancy fifteen days out and to be aware of vacant nights within the next fifteen days. You need these open nights to book. I recommend making manual price adjustments from your PriceLabs calendar every few days to discount open nights until they book. To make pricing changes on a particular day, click on the date, and change the dropdown selection for *Price* from *Fixed Price* to a *Percentage Decrease*. Start by setting open nights at -10 percent then -15 percent, and so on until all open nights within the next fifteen days are booked.

With only one listing, pricing adjustments can be handled in just a few minutes every other day, but with multiple listings, plan to spend approximately twenty minutes every day focused on near-term pricing for occupancy fifteen days out. This is the business management activity that provides you the most control over your success in the short-term rental arena. If you are concerned the nightly rate is too low, remember that you are balancing revenue with occupancy. You want to keep your short-term rental booked.

> **Pro Host Tip:** If you invest a small amount of time every one to two days adjusting the near-term pricing of your listing for occupancy and allow PriceLabs to generate your long-term pricing, you will maximize your revenue and be more successful than 95 percent of hosts on the planet. This is how the magic happens.

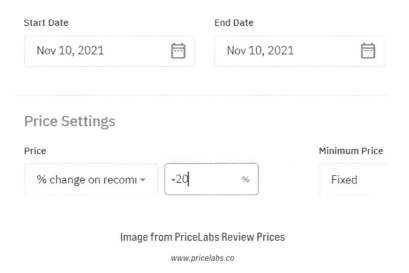

Image from PriceLabs Review Prices

www.pricelabs.co

Avoid the pitfall of thinking that your listing is worth $300 per night every night of the week and every month of the year. It is worth what a guest is willing to pay for it, given the number of guests to whom your listing is exposed. In the near term, you have a limited number of guests looking to book your space. However, if you keep your occupancy rate above 90 percent, you will be exposed to more guests in the future who are less price-sensitive and are willing to pay, say $500 per night, or more.

Airbnb rewards highly booked listings that garner more views.

So discounting in the short-term has multiple benefits. By taking a booking priced lower than usual, your listing still generates revenue. Selling two near-term nights for $100 per night will pay your utilities. More importantly, you will be gaining more views for your listing for future dates that will have higher rates. This is how dynamic pricing coupled with some manual near-term pricing adjustments propel a listing to the top of search results and revenue maximization. Also, if your listing is highly booked but is available for the dates a traveler wants to stay, it will show them a "Rare Find" badge. Airbnb uses this badge to highlight your listing and encourage guests to book quickly.

Tools such as PriceLabs help with year-round occupancy. Accept when the software suggests pricing down certain nights in certain months. You must let go of your personal opinion of what your rental is worth. Some nights, it might be worth $89, but if you keep your calendar full, you will be rewarded by the Airbnb algorithm. This means your lower-priced nights will end up creating more views for the higher-priced nights in your higher-priced seasons. Remember, your property cannot generate income when it is vacant.

Do not be afraid to charge higher prices than other listings in your market. In my experience, the more you charge, the fewer guest hassles you encounter. I don't have any science to support this, only the observations I've made working in this industry for the last six years, but I can say this: when you charge more, you attract more respectful guests. Perhaps it's the marketing placebo effect, or maybe it's a similar kind of mindfulness that comes with treating something more valuable with more care, in the same way one might drive an expensive car more carefully.

The Value of Opening Your Calendar

One of the keys to getting the maximum profit out of your short-term rental investment is to open your booking calendar for a twelve-month period. Many investors and hosts only keep three or four months of their rental calendar open for booking at any given time out of fear that they will under-anticipate demand and will get booked at lower rates.

If you are using dynamic-pricing software, keeping your calendar closed past three months is the best way to *not* receive the highest booking rates. Remember, your listing is worth what someone is willing to pay. Think about this scenario: my wife's birthday is October 1. As a good husband, I am not going to wait until September 15 to book a getaway for us. I am going to book a place six to twelve months out and book the nicest place available. If that place happens to be $400 per night, I am price insensitive, because it is my wife's birthday. Guests are price insensitive for birthdays, anniversaries, holidays, graduations, and other momentous events.

One of my major business breakthroughs occurred when I let PriceLabs take over my pricing instead of relying on my own self-limiting beliefs. You will be amazed at what someone is willing to pay to stay in your short-term rental.

My most recent short-term rental acquisition is a $320,000 custom-built cabin. The typical owner of this rental cabin would set a static rate of $350 per night each day of the week and each month of the year. In this scenario they would be leaving money on the table.

Let's take a look at this cabin's February 2022 rates set by PriceLabs. February is the lowest month for rental demand in my market. You will see an average weekday rate of $250 per night in February. Notice the dramatic difference in weekend rates. They are as high as $828 per night. Why are these weekend rates so high? The Valentine's Day and Presidents' Day holidays are driving guest demand, and PriceLabs has adjusted my prices accordingly.

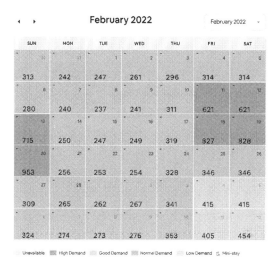

Copyright Ten:Eleven Press

An $800+ night listing. This concept is powerful. This is why we are looking around the corner when it comes to investing in short-term rentals. I paid $320,000 for a cabin that will potentially generate $10,876 of gross revenue in its slowest month. This is the power of investing in short-term rentals to generate financial freedom.

How are return rates like these possible? You are not crossing your fingers and hoping to rent your place a few weekends a month. You are making strategic decisions for pricing and occupancy based on the goal of feeding the Airbnb algorithm. Additionally, you are using tools designed to amplify your success.

→ Chapter 8 Takeaways ←

- Airbnb functions as a search engine. This means an algorithm determines which listings are shown in what order.
- The Airbnb algorithm values views, click-throughs, viewer engagement, and conversions to bookings from your listing. The better you are at generating those consumer actions, the higher your listing will show in guest searches.
- Pricing for occupancy is a concept that encourages the use of dynamic pricing to keep your calendar 90–95 percent full each month, which feeds the Airbnb algorithm.

9. STREAMLINING OPERATIONS AND BUILDING YOUR DREAM TEAM

Auto Messaging

As you launch your new Airbnb listing, guest communications and messaging quickly become hyper important. We live in an era of instantaneous consumer demand. Guests who have a question about your property want to hear back from you immediately. Make them wait too long, and they will book another property.

New hosts are justifiably worried about how much time they will spend messaging guests. Fortunately, there is a $25 per month tool called Hospitable (formerly known as Smartbnb) that automates guest messaging for hosts. You can choose to use their message templates or customize them to meet your needs. Hosts only write these messages once, and then you never have to worry if you have missed responding to an inquiry or booking opportunity. Hosts and guests both win in this highly responsive scenario.

As a host, if you are at work, at the gym, or out to dinner when a guest inquiry comes in, using Hospitable means you do not have to stress about immediately responding. A potential guest inquires about your listing on Airbnb, and Hospitable immediately sends a message back. Guests love receiving instant responses. Not only do guests appreciate prompt responses, the Airbnb algorithm also measures and rewards host response times, factoring them into your ranking.

I firmly believe that automated messaging contributes to guests selecting my properties instead of other properties whose hosts may take several hours or days to get back to them. Even when the guest books a reservation as a host using Hospitable, you do not have to do anything. Hospitable automatically sends the guest an email confirming and thanking them for their reservation.

I advise setting up eight automated messages. You will need to create content and timing rules in Hospitable for the following events: a new booking inquiry, a new request to book, a new reservation, guest check-in, cordiality/guest happiness check, reviewing a guest on Airbnb, and prompting a guest for an Airbnb review. I also have an automated message to follow up on expired guest inquiries.

For guests who send an inquiry about my properties, I use the standard inquiry template offered by Hospitable. It is a brief message stating that their dates are available and that I would love to host them. There is also a suggestion to book quickly so that no one else books the desired dates.

My New Booking Inquiry Template

Hello %guest_first_name%,!

Thank you for your interest in Shenandoah Gem ~ Sauna ~ Walk to River ~ King Bed for your trip in Luray!

I wanted to confirm right away that it would be a pleasure to host you from %date%

Although the cabin is still available at this time, I may have received requests for those dates. I would advise you to book quickly.

If you need any additional information, please feel free to ask, it would be my pleasure to answer you!

I look forward to hosting you!

My New Request to Book Template

Hello %guest_first_name%, and thanks for your interest in %listing_name%!

I wanted to confirm right away that I have received your request to book my %listing_type% from %check_in%, with %guests% for %nights%.

I will review your requests and respond to your specific questions as soon as possible so that you can plan your trip accordingly.

%answers%

If you need any additional information, please do not hesitate to ask, it would be my pleasure to answer you!

As you write your custom message for new reservations, give information that will help your guest plan their trip. Act as a travel planner and highlight your favorite places to visit, eat, hike, bike, and enjoy around your listing. If you have purchased your short-term rental in a place you love, this should be an easy message to create. If you invested in an area that is new to you, spend time discovering a few favorite places and feel free to incorporate Trip Advisor recommendations for the area. Remember, the more information you give your guests in this message, the fewer questions they will need to ask.

My New Reservation Template

Hello %guest_first_name%, and thanks for your reservation!

Here is some information to help you plan your cabin trip. Check-in time is after 3:00 PM on your arrival date, and check-out is at 11:00 AM on your departure date. Should you have any questions about our cabin or the surrounding area, I would be happy to answer them.

To Do In and Around the Cabin:
Our cabin has many fun items scattered throughout, so feel free to dig around for DVDs, cooking supplies, cards, games, hiking trail guides, books, magazines, coffee maker, and plenty of clean sheets and towels.

There is good cell phone reception, satellite internet service, and a collection of 100+ DVD's for guests to use. And feel free to bring your own.

What to do in town:
Downtown is dotted with quaint shops, small restaurants, and art galleries.

- The Warehouse Art Gallery is a family favorite, with everything from chairs made out of belts to local watercolors and pottery.
- The Valley Cork is a nice place to stop for wine and a cheese board.
- Gathering Grounds has fantastic coffee, baked goods, breakfast and more.
- West Main Market is the perfect spot for gourmet made-to-order hot and cold sandwiches and soup. Their roast beef and bleu cheese sandwich is a family favorite.
- Triple Crown BBQ is a roadside stand across from Walmart. Their BBQ is fabulous! Pick it up to go, or sit at one of their outdoor tables. *They tend to sell out by early evening, so go for lunch.
- Anthony's Pizza is our favorite hole-in-the-wall restaurant. Tucked in the strip mall one over from Walmart, they make stellar pizza, calzones, cheese steaks, and more. If you're into pasta, the Italian Combo" of lasagna and alfredo is our son's favorite.
- he Mimslyn Inn restaurant has a very nice Sunday brunch and serves dinner on select evenings.

The Luray Rescue Zoo is fantastic. And if you call the owner Mark, he will arrange to give you a behind the scenes tour complete with tiger feeding and porcupine petting for $25/person.

Luray Caverns is not only caverns but also a garden maze, rope course, and a number of small shops/museums to explore.

Mockingbird Spa - A cute little spa in the mountains. Book a massage with Kris... she's lovely!

Shenandoah River Outfitters offers tons of fun on water. Self-guided excursions include tubing, white water rafting, and canoeing. Feel free to pack a picnic and cooler for your float down the river.

Hiking & Biking - www.nps.gov/shen/planyourvisit/hiking-safety.htm

Lion's Tail Trail - a great little hike/path dotted with animal facts for kids and a pond. In early spring the pond is completely full of tadpoles.

Chasing Waterfalls – www.skylinedriveoverlooks.com/shenandoah-national-park-skyline-drive-waterfalls/

Skyline Drive – Absolutely amazing
www.nps.gov/shen/planyourvisit/driving-skyline-drive.htm

Local Wineries, Breweries, and Distilleries - www.discover-shenandoah.com/whisky-wine-loop/

Trip Advisor - Ranked top activities in Luray
www.tripadvisor.com/Attractions-g60964-Activities-Luray_Virginia.html

Five days before your arrival date, I will send you check in details and the front door lock code. Please make sure that your reservation reflects the correct number of guests who will be staying.

Please let me know if you have any questions. I love helping guests make the most of their trip!

Five days before check-in, guests should receive a customized, automated message. This message should include the property address, directions, door code, wifi login, and suggestions for local spots to stop at on their way to your listing. We receive rave reviews for guiding our guests to these small places, as well as activities and restaurants to consider during their stay. I feel great supporting local businesses, and my guests love receiving insider tips that make their trip more authentic and fun.

My Check-In Message Template

Dear %guest_first_name%,

Here is the check in information for your upcoming stay at our Mountain Top Retreat cabin. Please let me know if you have any questions as you plan your stay or upon arrival. I am very responsive to Airbnb messages.

The cabin is located at 1234 Sample Drive Luray VA – GPS or Waze should take you right there.

You can check in anytime after 3:00 PM and check out time is 11:00 AM to allow time to clean the cabin between guests.

The front door is secured with a digital deadbolt. Enter code <xxxx>. Then turn the deadbolt knob.

We have just upgraded the wifi. The network is named <xxxx>, and the password is <xxxx>.

As you drive into Virginia, you might enjoy a few local food gems on the way to our cabin.

In the town of Linden, the Apple House has rockstar apple cider donuts.They pour local cider into the batter, and when they're warm...wow!

15-20 minutes down the road in Front Royal, Two Fat Butchers has fantastic bacon and house-ground sausage (it's in a strip mall on the left side of the road). Across the street just past McDonalds is Spelunkers. They have stellar cheeseburgers, cheese steaks, and frozen custard. This is not fast food, so keep that in mind if you are in a hurry.

*During inclement weather such as snow or ice you may be required to have 4-wheel drive or tire chains. We also recommend purchasing travel insurance during winter months. We do not give refunds for road conditions that are out of our control. You have booked a secluded mountain cabin accessed by a moderately steep, bumpy gravel road.

Please take your trash with you as it cannot be left outside because it attracts the wildlife. If you are traveling on Route 340 there are two public trash/recycling centers where you can drop off and trash.

If you would like to build a fire, there is plenty of wood in the outside firebox. Please make sure to open the flue before starting the fire, and close it again before you leave.

Grocery Stores:

You can buy groceries at the Walmart located on 211 just past the Luray caverns. The store is open 24 hours per day. You can also shop at the Food Lion grocery store in the adjacent shopping center.

Should you have any questions, please feel free to message me.

It is both thoughtful and a good host practice to create a first morning hospitality email. Guests staying at your listing should receive an email checking to make sure they have settled in happily. I send Hospitable's stock response twenty-four hours after they check in. This message gives guests the feeling that I sincerely care about them and their stay. It also gives them the opportunity to voice any concerns, so I can fix them immediately instead of after receiving a poor review.

My Guest Hospitality Template

Hi %guest_first_name%,

We hope that you have settled in happily and that you are enjoying our cabin. Please let me know if there is anything you need or if we can assist you in any way!

All the best and enjoy your time in Luray!

If a potential guest has inquired about one of my cabins but their booking inquiry has expired twenty-four hours after my pre-approval, I have an automated message set to send after the expiration. This follow up reminds the person of their interest in my cabin and nudges them to book or ask any questions that may be keeping them from booking.

My Follow Up on Expired Inquiry Template

Hi again %guest_first_name%,

I hope this message will find you well. I see that my earlier pre-approval has expired. If you are still interested in renting out the cabin, please let me know.

Also, let me know if you have questions!

Best regards,

Culin

You can also use Hospitable to automate your guest reviews. As a host with many listings, I can attest that writing one-off reviews for each guest consumes a considerable amount of time. Reviewing guests on Airbnb is important, because your review sends a prompt for the guest to leave a review for your listing.

I have the software set up to submit a customized 5-star review twenty-four hours after a guest checks out. That twenty-four-hour window gives me time to stop that automated review if my housekeepers call me to report major guest-related issues.

On the topic of reviewing guests, remember you are running a business. Do not take things personally. You are going to host many guests, 99 percent of whom will be awesome guests and 1 percent of whom will be annoying guests. Occasionally you will host a couple of bad guests. If a plate gets broken or someone does not like your art choices, that is simply part of doing business. Do not leave them a bad review. I have left four bad reviews out of over 1,500 guest stays. Only if blatant disrespect to the property is evident do I feel the need to warn other hosts via a poor review.

My Guest Review Template

%guest_first_name% was a great guest! I'd be happy to host %guest_first_name% again anytime. %guest_first_name% took great care of my %listing_type%, left it clean and tidy, and was a pleasure to speak with. Highly recommended!

Guest reviews are incredibly important to your listing's position and success. So, outside of Airbnb's review email to guests, I also send my own message asking for a review.

My Review Prompting Template

Hi %guest_first_name%,

It was a pleasure hosting you in Luray. We will be certain to leave a great review for your stay and I hope you will have great trips again on Airbnb. If you ever come back, please let us know and give us the chance to accommodate you again!

If you ever have any suggestion on how to improve your trip, please do not hesitate to let us know right here, as we are constantly working to improve the experience for everyone.

Automating your standard messages makes your guests feel valued and cared for. Through this automation, your only day-to-day message responsibility is answering one-off questions, such as "Do I need to bring charcoal for the grill?" As a host, you can anticipate spending 5–10 minutes each day on guest messaging. Use your lunch break or toilet time to check the Airbnb app and send any non-automated messages.

Housekeeper

A stellar housekeeper is the most important member of your Airbnb team. They are your most important business partner. Find someone who truly cares about the property and loves providing a perfect guest experience instead of "just cleaning." Their dedication to their job and your property is paramount for the happiness of your guests and the success of your short-term rental. A dirty house always equals a bad review.

Cleanliness is a major driver of guest satisfaction. When people walk in and see that a rental is sparkling clean, they immediately have a positive outlook on your place. If something minor is not perfect during their stay, guests tend to overlook it. Conversely, if guests walk into a poorly cleaned house, they start with a negative attitude which can build into a bad review if anything else is less than perfect during their stay.

I have had tremendous success using yard signs to find house-keepers. Print high-quality yard signs though a service like Vistaprint with a Google Voice number and place them at the entrance to your listing's neighborhood. The quality of the sign indicates the high quality of the property and job position, making it enticing. Within two minutes of placing my first sign out for one of our cabins I had a phone call. I received eight more calls that evening. The quality yard sign method works because it catches the attention of house-keepers already working in your area, as well as neighbors who know individuals looking for more houses to clean.

Copyright Ten:Eleven Press

Another way to find a housekeeper is to post a job listing on indeed. com. Several of my mentees have used this popular worldwide job platform. With over 250 million unique visitors every month, indeed.com offers a digital way to connect with housekeeping professionals in your area.

Plan on conducting several interviews and pay attention to what each applicant has to say. If he or she has worked in hotels or is solely employed as a housekeeper, those are indicators of a true professional. Always ask what an applicant's backup plans are for vacation and sick days. Many times, they have relatives, colleagues, or helpers on call who can fill in for them. Once you have selected your primary housekeeper, keep a list of the top applicants to use as alternates in case of emergency, or if your first choice does not end up working out. Our favorite housekeeper vacuums the pillows on the couch. That does not happen in our house! As a guest, if you are worried about the cleanliness of a place, seeing vacuum lines on pillows will make you feel at ease.

During your interviews clearly determine if you or the housekeeper will be providing cleaning supplies. If you are the supplier, create a list of the supplies and touch base with your housekeeper monthly to learn what needs to be replenished. Plan to budget $100 to $200 per month in cleaning and household supplies. My budget analysis shows that I spend $100 monthly on my two-bedroom properties, $150 on my three-bedroom properties, and $200 on my four-bedroom properties. Below are two sample checklists that cover the minimum supplies. Feel free to add whatever you deem necessary for your short-term rental and guests.

Sample Cleaning Supply Checklist

Floor cleaner/disinfectant
Multi-surface spray
Toilet cleaner
Lysol
Windex
Furniture polish
Draino
Dish soap
Dishwasher detergent pellets
Laundry detergent

Fabric softener

Sponges

Swiffer duster replacements

Magic erasers

Garbage bags

Bathroom trash can liners

Oven liners

Sample Household Supply Checklist

Toilet paper

Paper towels

Shampoo

Bodywash

Soap

Hand soap refill

Coffee

K cups (for Keurig)

Coffee filters

Tea

Sugar

Creamers

Popcorn

Welcome snacks

In the vein of streamlining operations, I suggest creating your monthly cleaning calendar as a Google document. This ensures that any change you make, such as adding new guest bookings or removing bookings due to cancellations, can be seen by your housekeeper. As a host, it is not uncommon to experience a 10–20 percent cancellation average. This is due to many guests booking 30–90 days in advance and then having a change in plans. Communicating this volume of cancellations by phone or text would be tedious. Using Google documents means you only need to make one manual update regarding a cancellation and all housekeepers see it.

Set an expectation with your housekeeper that he or she will check the cleaning calendar daily. This will help prevent missed cleanings due to reservation changes and cancellations. Agree that guests encountering an uncleaned space is considered a failure on both of your accounts. It is also wise to agree on an emergency plan. Ideally, your housekeeper will commit to immediately rectifying a missed cleaning by arriving at the property and cleaning as soon as the mistake is discovered or at the convenience of the guests. In the event that your housekeeper is unable to take care of a missed cleaning, you have your list of back up housekeepers as a resource.

Operation Costs

Gross revenue minus all expenses related to your short-term rental equals your net revenue. Understanding monthly operating costs can help you forecast your short-term rental net revenue. Typical monthly costs include your mortgage, property taxes, insurance, electric bill, internet bill, cable TV bill, cleaning fees, cleaning supplies, yard maintenance, minor household goods replacements, and small repairs.

Housekeeping

Curious how much to pay your housekeeper? I have a two-tiered payment structure based on standard cleaning and extra cleaning. A standard cleaning is if one of the two bedrooms are used. An extra cleaning is if both/all bedrooms are used or if the guests left the place in poor condition. Feel free to work out whatever is best for you and your housekeeper, but be sure that it is fair. Remember, this person is the key team member to ensuring your guests are happy and your reviews are glowing.

Let's dive into the topic of paying your housekeeper. In a normal turnover, your housekeeper will spend two or three hours cleaning, changing linens, and doing laundry. I pay approximately $25 an hour, and I end up with fixed rates for each cabin. I pay $60 for my two-bedroom cabins with queen beds and $70 for my two-bedroom cabin with a queen bed and bunk beds.

Bunk beds are great for hosts because we can fit more guests in a room. However, they are a pain for housekeepers, as they involve an extra set of linens to clean and are difficult to remake. Pay your housekeeper more when he or she does more. I give all of my housekeepers the option to note a turnover as an extra cleaning. This means there were extra guests, a dog that shed everywhere, or a really big cleaning job. I pay $25 more for cleanings marked as extra.

It is also wise to use Zelle or Venmo to pay your housekeeper on a weekly basis. This saves you the hassle of writing checks and pays your housekeeper immediately, which will set you apart from his or her other cleaning clients.

Landscaping

Another expense to anticipate is lawn maintenance. A small amount of grass is a nice guest amenity. I pay $50 to have the yards at each of my properties mowed every other week. I have opted to forgo purchasing investment properties that have acres of lawn to maintain. Large, grassy yards are too much hassle for me as a host and detract from net revenue.

Snow removal is another potential expense to consider. These costs vary dramatically based on your location. If you are buying a short-term rental in an area that typically enjoys a moderate winter season, snow removal should not be a huge expense. If your listing is in a neighborhood, there is typically a community member who will plow the neighborhood. Be sure to put a disclaimer in your automated check in message that encourages guests to purchase travel insurance during winter months and specifies that you do not issue refunds for weather-related cancellations.

Internet

Decent internet is critical to the guest experience. Today, most people use the internet not only for work but also for streaming movies and entertaining their children. My advice is to invest in the best internet available in your area. My cabins are located in remote areas, so ground-based internet is not an option. I use HughesNet (satellite internet) and Blazing Hog (4G LTE) as service providers, with Star Link (satellite internet operated by SpaceX) on order for when it becomes available. Both internet services have a monthly rate of $125. Wherever you are, there is a solution. Ask your neighbors about their experience and choices of internet providers, and of course, do some online research for solutions.

Other Dream Team Members

Next up is building a team of service providers, plumbers, electricians, painters, landscapers, and snow removers. Don't know where to start? The key to being a successful real estate investor is to be an adept problem solver. The best way to find these professionals is to ask your new housekeeper for recommendations. If you are in a rural setting, most people who live in the area know who does a good job.

Create a Google document of all suggested professionals, along with their phone numbers and full names. Then head to the local hardware store to source additional names and numbers for each area of expertise. Ask the person in charge at the store for their recommendations and also look to see if business cards are posted on a bulletin board. Your goal should be to amass a pool of three or more professionals to call for any given situation. Cultivating this list will make your day-to-day management much easier. Trust me: the worst time to try to find a plumber, handyman, or electrician is during a guest emergency.

Remote Property Management

Many first-time hosts are curious if they should invest in a short-term rental near where they live, so they can be nearby and available for managing the property and handling emergencies. My answer to this question is twofold.

First off, I love to go to my places. I spend a couple days per month or per quarter staying at each property to make improvements, organize, and keep them in 5-star review shape. It is easier to spend time on your rentals if you live near them and enjoy the area. Remember, short-term rentals are made perfect every three days or so. This is very different from long term rentals where a property is untouched for a year, or more and then requires the investor to go in and make major repairs.

That being said, I spent a year living in Greece with my family while being a host for my eight properties. Despite a seven-hour time difference and living more than 5,000 miles away from my rentals, I was able to manage them easily. We had one issue the entire year, which was a power outage that I had no control over.

You can absolutely invest in a short-term rental that is further from where you live. You will just need to set up some systems to ensure your success. First, employ a great team of housekeepers and contractors. Then invest in someone to conduct quarterly owner's eye inspections and report back to you. When I was in Greece, my father-in-law did inspections for us. As a retired engineer, he was great at fixing things, reporting on conditions, and providing suggestions that would not have crossed our housekeeper's radar or been seen during a turnover day.

Just like in any other business, you are only as strong and successful as the team you build. Hire and contract with great people and pay fair rates. Keep your vendor relationships positive and professional. Give your housekeepers bonuses and or a basket of treats during high season and holidays, typically equal to the value of one cleaning. Also actively encourage and reward feedback from your team. Sending thank-you notes is another great way to show your appreciation for the professionals who keep your guests happy.

> OMGoodness I appreciate the card Danielle, it makes me want to try even harder to keep our guests happy. I enjoy my job and I hope it shows.
> I appreciate you guys also.
> Have a blessed upcoming thanksgiving..and always. 😉

→ Chapter 9 Takeaways ←

- Guest messaging is a critical task for hosts, both during booking conversations and to ensure guest satisfaction throughout a stay.
- Automating standard messages with a software tool like Hospitable saves hosts time and provides instant responses to guests.
- Creating a dream team of professionals will help you manage your short-term rental from a distance.
- Your most important hire is your housekeeper!

→ Tools & Technologies ←

Hospitable is a software that centralizes and automates guest messaging through the Airbnb platform for one or more short-term rental properties.

10. RISK MANAGEMENT

Have you ever heard the expression "take the risk or lose the chance"? With every new venture comes a certain amount of risk. And mitigating risk makes it easier to take the chance. Understanding the potential risks associated with short-term rental investing and taking appropriate preventative measures will help you run your rental more smoothly and sleep better at night.

Insurance

The main purpose of insurance is to reduce financial uncertainty and make accidental loss manageable. Short-term rentals are a niche industry that normal homeowners insurance is not designed to cover. This makes it imperative to obtain a short-term rental insurance policy to cover any major issues or accidents that relate to your short-term rental property.

Major insurance companies are beginning to catch up to the needs of short-term rental hosts, but you should be diligent and take your time investigating available coverage. These companies may offer a home sharing endorsement that is written for a second home partially used as a rental.

It is important to note that insurance is regulated at the state level, so many insurance carriers will have different products available in different states. This variability is why you will need to speak directly to your agent and clearly state your intentions for the short-term business use of your property.

Proper Insurance is a company that specializes in the insurance needs of short-term rental hosts. Proper Insurance was founded by bed and breakfast owners and is underwritten by Lloyd's of London. The policy they offer is written as a commercial business policy and specifically includes the exposure types that a short-term rental owner may face.

Below are questions to ask potential insurance carriers:

- Does this policy specifically cover business use as short-term rental property?
- Am I covered by this policy if I own multiple Airbnb properties?
- Does this policy cover loss of short-term rental income in the event of property damage, and how is that loss of income calculated?
- If something happens such as a water leak when the property is vacant, does this policy cover that damage?
- Does this policy provide coverage if a guest is injured while renting my property but is not on the property when the injury occurs?
- What is the policy coverage for rebuilding the home in the case of a total loss?

Property Risk Management

Do you have concerns about guests having parties at your property? Are you anxious about potential property damage? This is a common worry for new hosts. Fortunately, there are many tools available to help you protect your short-term rental.

Digital locks deliver more than just guest ease at check-in. They are also an important facet of guest safety and property security. Depending on the brand you purchase, digital locks can provide you with the ability to change codes after each guest stay or after entry by contractors. Additionally, some brands allow you to establish several different codes so that you can assign a separate, standing code for more regular service professionals, such as your house-keeper. This way, no one can access your property without your express permission via a code.

Equipping your property with smoke detectors and fire extin-guishers is an excellent way to protect your guests and your property from fire damage. We have smoke detectors installed on every floor of each of our cabins. We also keep a fire extinguisher in the kitchen and mounted next to all outdoor grills.

A $20 outdoor fire extinguisher saved one of our cabins from a grill fire. While a section of the cabin exterior wall was blackened, our guests were able to put out the fire before tremendous damage was done. Our guests were kept safe, and we were able to apply stain to the logs and replace the grill before the next guests checked in. That fire extinguisher literally saved a $300,000 investment.

Surveillance cameras are another way to keep an eye on your short-term rental property. Cameras can infringe on guest privacy. So if you choose to add a camera to your space, be certain you are compliant with Airbnb's rules. This way you can protect your property and also ensure that your guests' privacy is maintained.

Airbnb requires hosts to disclose if they are recording any part of a property. Hosts are also prohibited from using surveillance devices in bedrooms and bathrooms. Unless you have a unique circumstance, there are many other ways to safeguard your property without using a camera.

We only have a camera at one property, which is on a remote mountain top. The motion camera is installed at the peak of the roofline to provide a view of the driveway. This allows us to monitor snow conditions, housekeeper arrival/departure times, and the number of cars parked in the driveway. Guests are made aware of the camera on our Airbnb listing, and we have not had any complaints regarding it.

Ring doorbells are a more generally accepted way to monitor the entrance of your short-term rental unit. These devices are mini motion-activated cameras that record a brief video of motion at the door on which they are installed. Many consumers are familiar with these cameras, and guests understand that hosts are trying to keep abreast of who enters their property.

One downside of a Ring doorbell is that it must be wired into an electrical source when it is installed. Another issue is that you as a host may be inundated with motion messages as housekeepers, guests, contractors, and wildlife walk past the Ring doorbell.

Risk Management Technology

Managing the number of guests renting your property helps ensure guest satisfaction and reduces wear and tear on your space. As a host, you set the maximum occupancy number for your listing. What happens if your approved guests invite several more people to your property? How do you prevent a crowd from inhabiting or partying in your short-term rental? The answer is to use technological tools created to detect and alert hosts to the number of guests present in their property.

Party Squasher is a smart occupancy sensor. What is that? It is a tiny sensor that connects to your internet router and counts how many cell phones are present at your property. If you have a booking for two guests and Party Squasher sends you a message about twelve phones in your rental, you can reach out to the guest and inquire about the situation.

Guest noise level can be an issue for hosts, especially if your short-term rental is located in a building with several other units. Minut is a device designed to monitor noise decibel levels. Users can establish a threshold noise level and will then receive reports if that threshold is crossed, including how high the noise level was and how long it lasted. This information allows you to communicate factually with noisy guests and with any neighbors who may complain.

Are you concerned about guests smoking in your short-term rental and ruining its freshness for future guests? Technology to the rescue again! FreshAir is a device that detects smoking of any kind in your property. Simply plug FreshAir into an outlet. If it senses smoke, it will connect to your wifi and immediately send you an email report. FreshAir can detect cigarette and marijuana smoke, giving you as a host the ability to contact your guests if they break your house rules.

One of the most effective and lowest tech ways to safeguard your short-term rental is to be on good terms with neighbors in the area. As I mentioned in Chapter 6, the best time to meet your neighbors is when you initially spend several days living in your new property. Proactively introduce yourself to neighbors and explain that you are a short-term rental host. Tell them that you want to be a good neighbor and make sure that your guests do not disrupt their peace. Then share your contact information. Most neighbors will happily call or text you if they see too many cars in the driveway, hear a party starting, or observe damage to your property.

With any form of technology or camera, do not be tempted to watch what your guests do. Instead, use technology as a safeguard for your property, and also for your guests. Privacy is a critical amenity. No one wants to feel watched or violated. If you have installed technological devices, disclose them in your listing and use them with an abundance of caution and integrity.

Risk Management through Airbnb

Spending time upfront understanding options available to you makes handling difficult guest and property situations easier. Aside from using physical and technological tools to protect your property, there are also ways to mitigate risk via the Airbnb platform.

The Airbnb Host Guarantee, recently renamed AirCover, offers protection against guests damaging your property or belongings during a stay. If the guests do not reimburse you, the guarantee may provide property damage protection of up to $1,000,000. The key word in this guarantee is "may." In our experience as hosts, if you do not have a security deposit activated in your Airbnb listing, it is very difficult to receive reimbursement from a guest or from Airbnb.

Back in Chapter 7, we advised setting up a security deposit when you create your listing. If you did not do this, it is wise to access the Policies and Rules section of your listing and add a security deposit. Guests are never charged this fee unless damages occur. In the event of damage by guests, you as a host can request that the guests reimburse you. If necessary, you can escalate to Airbnb support staff and can ask that they impose security deposit payment on your behalf.

Many hosts are anxious about keeping their Superhost status and worry that a bad guest review will cause them to lose this status. This fear can potentially put hosts in the position of guest extortion. In this scenario, guests will threaten hosts with a bad review unless they are given a refund for a stay that had no issues. We have never experienced guest extortion, but have read reports of it on host forums.

The best way to avoid guest extortion is to keep all messaging on the Airbnb platform. If a guest calls regarding an issue, speak with them by phone, but then summarize the call in a message to the guest through the Airbnb platform. For example, follow up a phone call regarding a cleanliness complaint with a message sent through the Airbnb platform, stating something like this: "I am so sorry to hear that you are unhappy with the cleanliness of the cabin. Our housekeeper prides herself on making the space sparkling clean for each guest. Could you please send me photos of what is concerning you?"

By documenting your immediate response and concern as a Host in messages, Airbnb support can see that the guest was not ignored. If the guest provides photos of a dirty toilet or refrigerator, you can compensate them with a partial refund. However, if the guest is trying to pressure you into an unwarranted discount, they will not be able to provide photos.

It is imperative to keep all payments within the Airbnb platform. This safeguards you and your guests from fraud. Never take a PayPal or cash payment for a stay at your property and never issue a refund on these platforms. Airbnb is hypersensitive to offline payments and can use them as grounds to delete your Host account and listing.

Some hosts have a fear of their listing being permanently removed from the Airbnb platform. This is highly improbable. But if you are a person who likes to prepare for worst-case scenarios, it is easy to keep your listing photos saved in a file and to copy your listing description and photo descriptions into a document. This way, should you ever need to recreate your listing, you will not be starting from scratch.

Financial Risk Management

The final area of risk to consider and manage as a host is financial risk. There are a few best practices to allay fears related to money and your short-term rental investment.

As your property begins to generate revenue, strive to save enough money to cover two to four months in mortgage payments. This financial cushion is there in the unlikely event that you go a significant period of time without guests renting your space. For what it's worth, the only time we have seen a dramatic decrease in guest stays has been during natural disasters and at the beginning of the COVID-19 pandemic.

Another way to insulate your short-term rental from financial risk is to maintain excellent accounting records. Consider using QuickBooks to document and manage your monthly revenues and to track all expenses related to your property. It is also a good idea to hire a professional accountant to oversee the filing and payment of all local, state, and federal taxes for your property.

As motivational writer William Arthur Ward shares, "The greatest hazard in life is to risk nothing." No investment is without risk, but you can be confident that you are not blind to the potential pitfalls and conceivable problems of short-term rental investing.

→ Chapter 10 Takeaways ←

- Investing in the correct short-term rental insurance product protects your property and you as a host.
- Many inexpensive technologies are available to safeguard your short-term rental property.
- Equip your property with smoke detectors, carbon monoxide detectors, and fire extinguishers.
- Keep all guest messaging within the Airbnb platform to ensure the facts are accurately documented if a refund is requested or if Airbnb support staff become involved.
- Mitigate financial risk by saving enough money to cover the mortgage payment of your short-term rental property for several months in the future.

→ Tools & Technologies ←

Ring doorbells are smart doorbells that connect to your home wifi network and send alerts when motion is detected or when an individual presses the doorbell button.

Party Squasher is an inexpensive device that gauges the number of people present in your rental by detecting the number of mobile phones connected to your wifi network.

Minut is a device that measures noise decibels within your rental, alerts you when guests arrive, and alerts you if your fire alarm activates.

FreshAir is a device that can detect cigarette or marijuana smoke within your property.

Quickbooks is an accounting software that helps you manage invoices and expenses, pay bills, and track cash flow.

11. NAVIGATING YOUR FIRST THIRTY DAYS LIVE—WHAT TO EXPECT, CHECK, AND CHANGE

Day One Through Day Fourteen

Hooray, your listing is live! Now what? Your first goal as a new host is to achieve a total of five 5-star reviews as soon as possible. Prior to having five reviews, Airbnb will not show your guest reviews on your listing. When your listing has no reviews, this indicates to future potential guests that your property is new and that you as a host are new. In this situation, new is not necessarily good.

The best way to obtain rapid 5-star reviews is through bolstering your listing in the following areas: calendar availability, attractive pricing, surprise and delight, and guest communications. Let's start with calendar availability. I always coach my mentees to have their property 100 percent ready for guests when they publish their listing. You do not want your listing to go live with the first week or two blocked off for last-minute preparations. Your goal is to have guests check in the day after your listing is available. This will jumpstart you toward getting those first five reviews.

Next, attractive pricing is a way to drive rapid bookings. Implementing discounted pricing of 10–20 percent for your first few weeks makes your listing more attractive to potential guests. People love to get more than what they paid for, so a lower price also plays into increased guest satisfaction, which translates into rave reviews.

Then, as bookings materialize, be ready to surprise and delight your guests. Your first ten stays are also critical to achieving super host status. This is the time to pull out all the stops when it comes to pampering your guests. Consider leaving out gift baskets, local jam, a bottle of wine, or other items that will take your guest experience over the top. Write welcome notes to your guests on stationery and have your housekeeper set them out with your surprise and delight items. Guests love to feel welcomed and valued, and their reviews will reflect this.

Finally, communication is the ultimate way to guarantee 5-star reviews. If you have not already installed the Airbnb app on your phone, do so now. The app makes keeping up with bookings and guest messaging convenient. Check in on your guests via the app and ask if they are enjoying their stay. Tell them you are a new host and would love any feedback about what they love and what areas could be improved. Ask them for a 5-star review and tell them how important it is to you. Most new guests enjoy being part of your start-up story.

Expect your first fourteen days on the Airbnb platform to be euphoric. Your hard work has paid off, your listing is ready, and you will start seeing bookings pour in. Airbnb will give you a fifteen-day boost as a new listing. This boost results in a higher ranking and more views. While this helps new hosts, it also allows Airbnb to test your ability to convert bookings. Enjoy this early success but be prepared to make changes when your boost comes to an end.

Day Fifteen Through Day Thirty

Day fifteen is a pivotal day as a new host. Your boost from Airbnb will taper, so it is time to evaluate where your listing stands on its own. Set a reminder on your calendar to check your listing rank on days fifteen, twenty-one, and thirty.

As discussed in Chapter 7, your rank is where your listing shows in comparison to other Airbnb listings in your area. It is an excellent benchmark for your listing's success. Use incognito or private browsing mode on your web browser to search Airbnb's site for the following: your location, next available dates, and ideal number of guests. Where does your listing show up? Is it on the first page of the search? The third page of search? Or the thirtieth page? Record your exact search rank placement, and then act accordingly.

If your listing is showing on the first page of results for your area, it is time to pop the champagne and celebrate. If the listing shows somewhere further down in the search, there is no need to panic, but you do need to make changes.

Here are some of the fastest ways to improve your listing's ranking: discount near-term pricing, change your cancellation policy, rearrange your photos, add amenities, and learn from your guest reviews. You can tackle these areas one at a time or simultaneously. The key is to be actively monitoring and adapting your listing elements with the goal of achieving that top spot in the search results for your area.

Another way to improve your ranking is to adjust your base pricing. If your calendar is not filling up, a high nightly rate is usually the culprit. Go into your PriceLabs account and check your thirty- and sixty- day occupancy levels. If your thirty-day occupancy is below 50 percent, lower your base price by $10 to $20. This small tweak will typically result in an influx of bookings, as Airbnb alerts guests who favorite your listing when there is a discount.

> **Pro Host Tip:** Do not get attached to a specific nightly rate for your listing. A place is worth what a guest is willing to pay for it on any given night. You may have a few low rates as you start out and during low season, but you will have jaw-droppingly high rates as your listing matures and during high season and holidays.

Changing your cancellation policy is another way to boost your listing's ranking. If you initially set your policy to strict or firm, consider loosening to a moderate cancellation policy that allows a full refund for cancellations within five days of the booking date. A flexible cancellation policy that allows cancellations twenty-four hours before check-in is even more attractive to guests with demanding work schedules, young children, or those coordinating a trip with friends or other family members. The easier your rental is to book, the higher Airbnb will place it in search results.

Rearranging your photo sequence is a quick and simple way to impact ranking. The first five photos in your listing are what viewers see when they first click through to your listing. Prioritize photos that show the best features of your short-term rental. Swapping your cover photo has the greatest impact on guest interaction. You want your listing to stand out from all of the other options on Airbnb, grab a guest's attention, and compel them to book so that they can have what they see. Photos of breathtaking views, outdoor amenities (i.e., a hot tub or beautifully furnished screened porch) or indoor amenities (i.e., claw foot bathtub or grand stone fireplace) should be in your first four photos.

Do not be afraid to audit your competitors. Scroll through the top listings in your area and take note of what they offer that you do not offer or that you do not emphasize. If your competitors have a fire pit, hammocks, or corn hole games, these are all easy amenities to purchase and add to your listing. Read competitor's reviews to see what guests most appreciate, and make sure that you are offering and doing the same things for your guests.

Finally, read your listing reviews and private feedback from guests. Resist feeling insulted or defensive regarding complaints or suggestions. Anything negative must be addressed to ensure a high ranking and the financial success of your short-term rental investment.

Attain Superhost Status

Mentees always ask me how to become a Superhost on Airbnb. It is a simple equation. Superhost status is attained by not canceling reservations and by having great reviews. Superhost status is evaluated and awarded four times per year. To qualify, you must host ten stays, have a twenty-four-hour response rate of over 90 percent, and maintain a 4.8 or greater overall review rating. Once awarded, a Superhost badge will be added to your listing and host profile.

Many people think, "If I achieve Superhost status, then Airbnb will recognize my status and will treat my listing preferentially." They assume that attaining Superhost rank will cause the Airbnb ranking algorithm to feature their listing higher in search results. This thinking is partially correct.

The factors measured by the Airbnb algorithm for Superhost status are actually what the algorithm uses to determine where your listing shows. So, striving for high occupancy, not cancelling guest stays, generating quick responses to guests communication, and receiving 5-star reviews will drive your listing upward in search ranks before you achieve Superhost status. You have several tools to ensure success for each of the measured factors.

Aside from algorithmic rewards for Superhost actions, there is also a consumer preference component. Many people—myself included—filter for Superhost listings when planning a trip. Why? Because guests know that Superhosts have great places, great reviews, great guest communication, and a strong commitment to guest satisfaction. The algorithm values what guests value, and the reward system ensures that hosts/listings that meet customer expectations are the first ones they see in a search.

Treat Your Airbnb As a Business

Your short-term rental is an investment. If you treat it like a hobby, it will be a side hustle with decent returns. If you establish your short-term rental as a business and treat it like one, you will be efficient with your time and able to maximize your returns.

Set up a QuickBooks account and separate bank account for your short-term rental. Then, link QuickBooks to your rental bank account so that your bank feeds pull all transactions into

QuickBooks. Next, open a debit and credit card to be used for all expenses related to your short-term rental. Do not use these cards for any purchases unrelated to your business.

Once you begin noticing monthly income in excess of your monthly expenses, it is wise to designate a second bank account to auto-deduct a set monthly amount to pay your quarterly estimated taxes before spending that excess money. Remember, this new income you are generating is taxable income (less expenses and depreciation). Consult your accountant or tax professional to estimate an accurate starting point for your tax allocation. Do not wait until the arrival of a tax bill on April 15 to think about saving!

As your short-term rental begins to generate income, avoid the urge to spend your profits. This income should cover the property mortgage and monthly expenses. You should also consider building cash reserves for monthly expenses and necessary improvements. Once those goals are met, your short-term rental income can be saved for your next property purchase, used to cover your primary residence mortgage, or used to replace you or your spouse's income.

A professional accounting software will make preparing your tax returns easier for your accountant. These softwares make it easy for you to provide your accountant with a copy of the company file that will include all of your revenue and expenses categorized by type. This saves your accountant time, and thus saves you money.

Consider creating a tracking sheet for your monthly revenue goals for your listing. On that sheet add a monthly goal column that lists how much you realistically want to earn each month from your short-term rental. Setting a goal is important. Ruth Henderson, Product Director of Alexon Group, says, "What gets measured gets done." You may have to adjust your goal based on seasonality, but knowing what you want to gross monthly will keep you focused and driven to achieve it.

	2021	2021	Year over Year
	Goal	Actual	Change
January	$6,400	$5,638	140.5%
February	$6,400	$3,518	15.9%
March	$6,400	$6,646	77.6%
April	$6,400	$6,699	172.9%
May	$6,400	$8,718	153.4%
June	$6,400	$9,140	42.7%
July	$6,400	$10,331	72.0%
August	$6,400	$8,806	20.7%
September	$6,400	$7,969	42.0%
October	$6,400	$10,471	22.7%
November	$6,400	$8,046	40.9%
December	$6,400	$8,596	47.4%

Housekeeping Review

After your listing has been live for thirty days, it is crucial to closely examine any guest feedback about cleaning. Cleanliness is the number one driver of guest satisfaction. You can have the most amazing Airbnb in the world, but if it is dirty, you will receive poor reviews.

Schedule a call or chat with your housekeeper. This is the perfect time to compliment him or her for any positive guest feedback and to bring up any suggestions from negative guest feedback. Use this conversation to emphasize how you and your housekeeper are a team, working together to create an amazing guest experience.

Ask your housekeeper for his or her input and advice for improving your short-term rental and inquire about any equipment or supplies they need to do an even better job. You will be surprised by the valuable ideas they share and by their excitement to be part of a team with a vision for creating the ultimate guest experience. If your team conversation and improvement suggestions are not met with enthusiasm, you may not have found your perfect cleaning partner.

A few years ago, we renovated a large cabin on top of a mountain. We replaced the floors, installed gorgeous furniture, outfitted multiple decks with fire tables, and hanging basket chairs, and Danielle painted all forty-seven doors and drawers to the kitchen cabinets. It was the nicest cabin we had ever created together. Unfortunately, that cabin struggled on the review front. Our housekeeper was doing the bare minimum, and our guests were underwhelmed. When we partnered with a new housekeeper, our reviews skyrocketed.

The first thirty days during which your short-term rental investment is published on Airbnb are particularly important. This is not the time to set it and forget it. Pay particular attention to making your first five guests happy and adjust your pricing to keep your occupancy rate high. Treat your rental like a business and set up a revenue tracking sheet to clearly measure monthly net income against your investment goals. The time and attention you spend in your early launch period will pay dividends for the rest of your short-term rental endeavor.

→ Chapter 11 Takeaways ←

- As you launch your short-term rental, focus on obtaining five 5-star reviews as quickly as possible.
- Strive to attain Superhost status by avoiding cancelling any guest reservations, responding to all messages within twenty-four hours, and maintaining guest reviews of 4.8 or higher.

- Treat your short-term rental property like a business by using QuickBooks to record all of your financial transactions.
- Monitor all guest reviews and private feedback related to cleaning, and conduct a meeting with your housekeeper to finetune your success strategies together.

→ Tools & Technologies ←

QuickBooks is an easy-to-use accounting software option that helps hosts keep track of all short-term rental expenses.

12. HOSPITALITY AND CUSTOMER SERVICE

Adopting a Customer Service Mindset

Congratulations! When your Airbnb listing is published, you as a host will have officially joined the hospitality industry. You are now in charge of guest relations and are managing a team of housekeepers and other service professionals. Your goal is to deliver a friendly and generous reception to each of your guests.

Creating the correct customer service mindset for yourself and your team will help you navigate guest communications, team mishaps, and circumstances beyond your control. Ritz-Carlton is considered the epitome of hospitality, so as hosts, we can learn a great deal from their company credo. The main takeaways from the Ritz-Carlton credo are prioritizing the genuine care and comfort of your guests, as well as fulfilling their unexpressed wishes and needs. These areas of focus should guide your customer service mindset. Inspired by the Ritz-Carlton, we created our own credo to help frame our mindset as hosts as well as the expectations of our team members:

The Host Coach Credo

Our properties are places where taking care of guests is our number one goal. We endeavor to provide unparalleled cleanliness, comfort, and attention to details that will both exceed our guests' expectations and delight them.

There are several Ritz-Carlton service values that are also worthy of adopting as an Airbnb host and team. Being responsive to expressed wishes and needs of guests, creating unique memorable experiences, continuously innovating and improving guest experiences, owning and immediately resolving guest problems, and bearing responsibility for uncompromising levels of cleanliness are all incredibly important hospitality concepts that will contribute to your success as a short-term rental host. Below are the service values of our team. Feel free to borrow them or create your own.

The Service Values of the Host Coach Team

- I strive to go beyond meeting the needs of our guests.
- I have the power and permission to make decisions that create a better experience for our guests.
- I have the power and ability to prevent and solve guest problems promptly.
- My thoughts and ideas are important and should be shared and received with enthusiasm.
- I am proud of my job, my services to guests, and the properties in which I work.
- I am responsible for doing my very best work to ensure clean and safe environments for our guests.
- I protect the privacy and property of my guests and employers.
- I have the opportunity to do my best every day and enjoy the satisfaction that comes from providing superior hospitality.

Airbnb Rating System

Airbnb does not have a host credo or a defined list of guest service values. However, they do have seven subcategories for guest reviews, which means these areas are important to both the company and to guests. Understanding the subcategories of accuracy, cleanliness, check in, communication, location, value, and amenities will aid your quest for great reviews and Superhost status.

Listing Quality > Guest Expectations = High Accuracy Reviews

During the review process, your guests will be asked to rate your listing on accuracy. What does this mean? Guests are asked if your online listing accurately represents your real-life listing. Guests are generally happy when your rental meets or exceeds their expectations. Guests are unhappy when your rental falls below their expectations. This is why we suggested in Chapter 6 that you take accurate photos of all rooms in your listing. Guests do not mind an older bathroom as long as they know about it before they book. Also, be sure that you accurately represent the location of your listing and its amenities. Transparency in all aspects is a policy that will boost accuracy reviews.

Listing Cleanliness > Guest Expectations = High Cleanliness Reviews

Cleanliness is the next subcategory guests will rate your listing on. I believe this is the most important subcategory for overall guest satisfaction. Airbnb has a list of cleanliness standards that include the following: making sure your space is free of mold and vermin, free of mildew in showers and excessive dust, and that cleanings occur between guest stays. Your goal is to ensure that your listing is sparkling clean every time a guest checks in.

Good Communication + Keyless Entry =
High Check-in Reviews

Check-in is another guest review subcategory. Communication and technology make this a very easy category to excel in. A smooth check-in experience sets the tone for your guest's stay. It is smart to invest in a digital lock for your short-term rental. Keyless locks remove the hassle of looking for a lockbox, losing keys, and guests locking themselves out of your listing. They also remove the need for someone to meet guests at a designated time to provide them with a key.

In your guest messaging, communicate that your rental has a keyless lock and that the code will be sent to the guest five days before check in. Then, message guests the door code five days before their arrival along with other standard check in information. If you are using an automated guest messaging tool, these emails can be set up to generate automatically so that you never forget to send them.

Automated Messages + Prompt Responses =
High Communication Reviews

Guests will also be asked to rate you on your communication as a host. Using automated messaging software, such as Hospitable, ensures that all standard messages are communicated in a timely manner. As a host, you are still responsible for promptly responding to any non-standard messages from guests. When you hear the Airbnb app chime, immediately check your messages and respond to your guests. If you need time to find the correct answer or solution for the guest, reply immediately and communicate that you are working on the answer for them. Guests simply want to be heard and to know that you as a host are available to help.

Accurate Location + Environmental Expectations = High Location Reviews

Believe it or not, your listing will also be rated on its location. Airbnb wants guests to receive an accurate understanding of where your listing is located and how close it is to local points of interest. It is also important to accurately describe your listing's environment. Set guest expectations as to whether your listing is secluded, whether it is exposed to street noise, or any other environmental considerations that would be helpful for guests to know ahead of booking.

Value > Price Paid = High Value Reviews

Value is another subcategory for guests to review. In this context, value equates to a guest's opinion on whether your rental was worth the price they paid for it. If you are charging high nightly rates, make sure that you blow your guests away with stellar communication, plenty of amenities, and surprise and delight items. Together, these factor heavily into a property's perceived value.

Accurate Amenity List + All Amenities in Working Order = High Amenity Reviews

Your listing will also be rated on its amenities. This does not mean you will receive low stars if you do not have a swimming pool. Rather, this subcategory is related to the amenities you advertise in your listing. As a host, you want to ensure that everything you promise to guests in your listing is in good working order. Setting this expectation with your housekeeper that they will check amenities during turnovers and will alert you to any issues is a great way to make sure your amenity score stays high.

Each of Airbnb's seven subcategories feed into the most important question posed to guests: "Rate your overall experience

at this listing." You are in the running for a 5-star rating if a guest
experiences all of the following: the listing description was accurate;
it was sparkling clean upon guest arrival; the check-in process was
smooth; you communicated efficiently as a host; the location met
expectations; the price was in line with the value of the listing;
and all amenities were functioning. Even if you were not perfect
in every category, a guest's overall experience is what determines
their starred review of your property.

Handling Guest Issues

It is impossible to participate in the hospitality industry and never
encounter issues. To err is human, and there are a lot of humans
involved in your Airbnb's success. The two most important factors
in any crisis situation are how you handle the problem and how
you treat the people involved.

There are three steps to handling a guest issue. First, listen to your
guest as they communicate the issue. Do not interrupt them with a
defensive answer or even with a helpful solution. Unhappy people
want the opportunity to be heard. Second, once your guest has told
you about the problem, acknowledge it. Apologize for the problem and
empathize with how that problem makes the guest feel. Finally, communicate with your guest about the best way to solve the problem.

It is important to offer your guest the resolution that works best
for them. You can suggest several options to solve the problem
they have encountered. For example, if the porch lights are burned
out, you can offer to send a service professional over to replace the
bulbs. Some guests will like this option, while others would prefer
to be issued a small refund and replace the light bulbs themselves.
Often, a guest simply wants to communicate an issue, and once you
empathize with them, they are no longer upset and do not require
an immediate solution. These guests will not want anything done
about the lights, so you can change them after they check out. By
giving your guests options, you allow them to select what will make

them happiest and salvage their stay.

As previously stated, it is best practice to conduct all of your communications through the Airbnb messaging platform. If you take a guest call, be sure to summarize the content of the call in a message sent through the platform, afterwards. This serves the dual purposes of keeping the guest abreast of all steps in the solution and providing documentation if Airbnb customer support gets involved.

Handling Cleaning Issues

Regardless of how amazing your housekeeper is, you will undoubtedly encounter cleaning issues. Calendars get mixed up, and mistakes happen. Guests are most upset when they walk into a space that has not been cleaned. Putting yourself in their shoes, it is easy to understand their discontent.

If you receive a message about a missed cleaning, respond with profuse apologies and an immediate cleaning fee refund. Depending on the time of day, offer to have your housekeeper come clean while the guests go out for a meal or engage in an outdoor activity. Most guests will be satisfied with this solution.

Some guests will volunteer to change the sheets themselves and will not want your housekeeper to intrude on their stay. Others will continue to vent their frustration about the situation. Give unhappy guests a refund equal to half or one night's stay. Continue to empathize with your guests and do whatever is necessary to make them feel better about the cleaning issue.

Early in my hosting experience, I failed to make guests who encountered a cleaning issue feel better about the problem. In hindsight, I should have voluntarily given them a larger refund or found a creative way to compensate for their disappointment. The guests' 1-star rating and multi-sentence review detailing how unclean the cabin was cost me thousands of dollars in lost bookings. I had to lower the nightly rates for my cabin in order to rebuild bookings until their review was eventually buried by glowing 5-star reviews. Learn from my mistakes and always go above and beyond to resolve cleaning issues for your guests.

Handling Issues Beyond Your Control

Your short-term rental can be sparkling clean with all amenities in perfect working condition, but factors outside your control can impact your guests' experience. Power, internet, and water outages are just a few of the factors that can disrupt a stay. While you cannot control these issues, you do need to plan for and deal with them as a host.

The best way to handle issues beyond your control is with rapid communication, honesty, and empathy. If a guest reports an outage, immediately message them that you are contacting the utility company. Next, message the guests with the expected outage time communicated by the utility company. Some guests will see a power, internet, or water outage as a minor inconvenience, while others will want to cancel their stay. As a host, allow your guests to do what is best for them in their situation. Offer to refund a night if they decide to leave early.

Planning for worst-case scenarios ahead of time can help you be the best host possible for your guests. Because our cabins are located in remote areas where fallen trees and storms can interrupt electricity, we have a specific cabinet dedicated to lanterns, flashlights, candles, and matches. Giving guests an immediate source of light helps keep them calm during a power outage. We have even had guests message that their kids thought playing games by candlelight was the best part of their stay. So, think about what outages could commonly occur where your short-term rental is located, and then create kits or fill a cabinet with items to help guests make the best of worst-case situations.

Refunds

When it comes to maintaining guest satisfaction, a small refund can go a long way. I always refund the cleaning fee for any minor inconveniences a guest reports. The refund makes the guest feel heard and shows that I care deeply about their experience. Sending a $60 refund because a guest ran out of toilet paper may seem crazy, but it is worth the money to ensure a good review.

If there is a problem with any major amenity, I immediately issue a refund valued at half the price of one night's stay. For instance, if a guest booked at $300 per night and encountered a hot tub that was not usable, I would refund them $150. I would then ask if they would like me to contact our service company to have a professional come troubleshoot the issue during their stay. A refund, coupled with an empathetic solution, is the best way to handle major guest complaints.

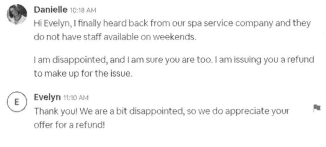

Danielle 10:18 AM
Hi Evelyn, I finally heard back from our spa service company and they do not have staff available on weekends.

I am disappointed, and I am sure you are too. I am issuing you a refund to make up for the issue.

Evelyn 11:10 AM
Thank you! We are a bit disappointed, so we do appreciate your offer for a refund!

Contacting Airbnb Support

If you encounter a situation where you have issued a refund, have attempted to resolve a guest problem, and still feel the guest is unsatisfied, it is time to call Airbnb Support. The purpose of Airbnb Support is to mediate guest and host situations through communication and refunds. By calling the Support team and explaining the situation, you can share facts about the issue, as well as the steps you have taken as a host to resolve the issue. This puts you in good standing if the unhappy guest calls the Support team afterwards.

Percent Dissatisfied

The concept of Percent Dissatisfied is important for hosts to understand. There is a small percentage of the population who are perpetually dissatisfied and who will always be unhappy with what they encounter. Most of your guests will be wonderful people who enjoy your space and leave 5-star reviews. Members of the Percent Dissatisfied club will not be happy with your space regardless of what ever you do. They will find as many issues to complain about as possible, including things outside of your control, such as the weather.

Do not allow the Percent Dissatisfied to get under your skin. In these times consider that it's purely business and you will deal with dissatisfied customers in any industry. Be kind, issue refunds, offer solutions, and hold your ground. You are not a doormat: you are a professional short-term rental host. Remind yourself that this, too, shall pass. The Percent Dissatisfied will check out, and lovely new guests will replace them soon enough.

Responding to Bad Reviews

Between human error, situations outside your control, and the Percent Dissatisfied, you will inevitably receive a bad review at some point on your journey. The manner in which you respond to this review is crucial. After reading a bad review, take a moment to digest it. Ask yourself which parts of the review are true and which parts are blown out of proportion. The best thing you can do is to write a thoughtful response that addresses the complaint and illustrates how you tried to solve the problem. It is important to avoid a defensive tone in your response and to keep it as simple as possible, as your response to the review will be visible to other potential guests.

Michael
July 2021

I was a little disappointed that the pond was not what I expected. I was looking forward
to fishing but the area was overgrown and not a good location to fish at.

Response from Culin
July 2021

Hi Michael, I'm sorry you didn't enjoy the neighborhood pond. Our son
loves to fish there. I am glad your private feedback said how clean the
cabin was and that you enjoyed the hot tub.

No matter how frustrated you feel, do not say anything negative about the guest in your public review. Take the polite high road. Think of it this way: you are not addressing this particular guest, you are writing for the benefit of future potential guests who will read the review. The good news is that guests can only post a public review. The Airbnb platform does not permit them to respond to your response and continue to tarnish your listing and reputation as a host.

Most future potential guests will see one poor review out of hundreds and will assume this to be an anomaly, realizing that either that guest or the situation was outside the norm. Your gracious and factual response as a host will show your dedication to hospitality and will signal that you are a reasonable individual. Guests want to book stays with reasonable hosts who can handle guest issues.

Once you have responded to the bad review, determine what you can do to prevent future poor reviews. If there was an issue with cleanliness, have a conversation about expectations with your housekeeper. If there was a complaint about bugs or rodents, hire a monthly pest control service. If an amenity was not functioning properly, have it repaired or replaced as soon as possible. Bad reviews are painful, but if you choose to learn from them, they offer a strong opportunity to improve your listing and make you a better host.

Do not let negative reviews tarnish your feelings about hosting. Instead, focus on the positive aspects of your short-term rental journey! Becoming an Airbnb host will change your life. You will develop keen hospitality skills and have the opportunity to share your favorite place with guests. Over time, you will be tandem to engagements, anniversaries, birthdays, graduations, and family holidays. As a host, you will also develop close relationships with your housekeeper, service professionals, and neighbors. Airbnb allows your community and skill set to grow exponentially.

→ Chapter 12 Takeaways ←

- Cultivate a hospitality mindset for yourself and your dream team as you serve your guests.
- Focus on providing excellent levels of cleanliness, communication, check-in ease, and functional amenities to ensure optimal guest reviews and ratings.
- Handle guest issues with grace. Do your best to promptly correct the problem and issue a partial refund if it is warranted.
- If you receive a bad review, learn from it and respond in a way that indicates your commitment to high hosting standards for future guests.

→ Further Reading ←

The New Gold Standard: 5 Leadership Principles for Creating a Legendary Customer Experience Courtesy of The Ritz-Carlton Hotel Company by Joseph A. Michelli

13. REVIEW, REINVEST, AND RENOVATE

As you progress in your short-term rental journey and your listing begins to generate revenue, do not simply sit back and relax. To maintain your success, you must focus on continuously improving your listing through reinvestment and responding to guest reviews.

Review Your Reviews

Public guest reviews of your property matter for many reasons. Great reviews will result in more bookings and a higher search rank placement for your listing on Airbnb. These reviews also help you identify what guests value most about your property and what aspects might need improvement.

Private feedback and less-than-5-star reviews are also very important to you as a host. As your listing goes live, be hyper focused on your reviews and adopt the mindset that negative reviews are not personal—they are intel! You need to know if an amenity is missing or broken and if your housekeeper is not doing a great job. Guest feedback and reviews will also alert you if some area of your property has been damaged by weather or by prior guests. Addressing complaints from private feedback or a poor review will help you improve your listing and ensure great reviews from future guests. Be sure to reply to the public review about an issue with a positive comment, indicating that you appreciate the feedback and have remedied the situation.

Second Round of Micro and Macro Amenities

As your short-term rental revenue starts to flow, consider earmarking some percentage of this money for purchasing additional micro and macro amenities for your property. You may have a running list of amenities you would like the property to pay for, or you can use information gleaned from reviewing your reviews to decide what to prioritize.

A hot tub is one of the best macro amenities you can add as a host for generating additional bookings and revenue. I conducted an analysis across all of my cabins and found that properties with hot tubs netted $900 more per month based solely on that amenity. This data helped us create a plan to save and reinvest cabin revenues to install hot tubs at every short-term rental we own.

Another macro amenity that generates more bookings and higher nightly rates is flooring. Changing out carpet for high-quality vinyl plank flooring, such as COREtec, can make a huge difference. New floors update the look of your rental and, perhaps more importantly, make it pet-friendly. Guests with pets are happy to pay a higher nightly rate so that their furry family members can travel with them. In fact, many of my mentees charge an additional fee of $25 to $100 per booking for pets. This is one more way to increase your listing's revenue.

Depending on the size of your yard, consider adding a screened-in gazebo, a premium outdoor yard game area, or a firepit with seating. You might also upgrade the dated outdoor furniture that may have conveyed with the property. Consider adding or replacing anything outdoors that would make a guest's stay more enjoyable. Your investment will be paid back with great reviews and increased bookings.

Exterior paint is an important amenity, although it may seem non-apparent, until you consider it for a minute. Guests book based on photos, and exterior photos are one of the first things they see in your Airbnb listing. You can absolutely launch your listing with dull exterior paint colors, but investing in fresh exterior paint that "pops" can dramatically impact booking potential.

The third cabin we acquired had a cute bungalow look with brown and gray paint. While the exterior colors were not our favorite, the place desperately needed new flooring, new kitchen cabinets, and interior paint. Those updates took budget priority.

A few years later, Danielle and I were spending a few days at that cabin and decided it was time to paint it. Instead of going with a gray and white theme, Danielle pushed for a dark blue exterior, white trim, and a yellow door. I hated the idea of a yellow door, as it is not consistent with our personal style. She persisted, and that cabin has seen a substantial increase in views and bookings. The cabin with the yellow door jumps out in listing photos and makes it easy for future potential guests to remember.

Inside your short-term rental, you may want to update an appliance, change the vanity in the bathroom, or trade out mediocre furniture with amazing furniture that has a "wow" factor. Whatever you decide to do, remember that these incremental investments are strategic. You are not wasting your profits: you are continuously improving your listing and, therefore growing its revenue generating potential.

> **Pro Host Tip:** If you add a macro amenity, consider updating your listing title to include it. This is one more way to advertise how great your listing is, and the new words feed the Airbnb algorithm. For example, if you have a hot tub installed on the deck, you could add the words "new hot tub" to the end of your listing title.

Renovations

It is wise to consider strategic renovations at this point in your short-term journey. Much like in the traditional real estate market, improvements to kitchens, bathrooms, and flooring yield the biggest financial rewards.

Our first cabin had Formica countertops and a terrible, dead rose–colored shower insert and vanity. When we were using it as a family getaway, those things did not matter. When we started renting out our cabin, updating these elements was not in the budget. We did our best with fresh paint and new furniture, planning to reinvest in the kitchen and bathroom at a later date.

Six years later, we blocked off a week to renovate the bathroom, paint the kitchen cabinets, install quartz countertops, and replace the carpet with COREtec vinyl planking. When these renovations were complete, we were able to designate the cabin as pet-friendly and increase our rates by $50 per night, thus generating $1,500 more per month. These renovations also resulted in the property's Airbnb overall quality rating rising from 4.78 to 4.9.

As you plan your renovations, it is important to consider all of the costs, including opportunity cost. Do not solely budget for contractors and materials; budget also for the time your short-term rental property will be off the rental market. We try to block off no more than five days for any renovation project. Keeping renovations contained within short windows of time protects occupancy rate and revenue generated from bookings, both of which impact your listing's search rank. You should also schedule an extra deep cleaning to remove any leftover dust and debris before your next guests arrive.

Finally, avoid the quicksand that is project creep. As you make one part of your property amazing, you will be tempted to add more and more things to the contractor's to-do list. Do not stray from your original plan. Hold yourself to a specific budget and timeline. Let guest revenue pay for further improvements.

My mentee William purchased his second short-term rental

property a year ago. He planned to complete a few minor renovations prior to listing and then use the property's rental revenue to reinvest in additional renovations a year later. It was a great plan that unfortunately spun out of control.

William and his spouse allowed more and more projects to be added to the pre-listing renovation plan. They went from a three-month renovation plan to one that took over twelve months. William has lost $100,000 in potential rental revenue, has gone well over his original budget, and has worked every weekend and holiday for the last eleven months. He is not having fun. I am not sure he will ever invest in another short-term rental. This is not because his investment will not generate revenue, but because he had such a miserable self-inflicted experience.

Quarterly Owner's-Eye Inspections

No one cares more about your short-term rental property than you do. You may have the world's best housekeeper and have received all 5-star reviews, but it is still critical to schedule quarterly inspections of your property.

Block off at least one night every four months to stay at your rental and perform an inspection. Check dishes for chips and check linens for snags or holes. Buy replacements for anything not in pristine condition. Organize the cabinets in the kitchen and any game shelves or children's toys. Bring spices and oils to restock the pantry. Look for and take care of any dusty baseboards or spider webs on ceiling fans or tall window treatments. Walk the yard and look for holes, fallen branches, dog poop, landscaping issues, and any exterior wear on the property and deck.

Give yourself grace as a host. Understand that you will not be able to fix everything you find in one night. Create and maintain an ongoing list of improvements that you can handle, as well as a list of tasks for your service professionals and lawn care person. The most important thing is to actively work to accomplish these lists. There is no value in making lists of needed improvements if you forget or neglect them.

It is also important to give your housekeeper grace. Completing turnovers within the short window of time between guests is very different from spending a full day on a deep clean. Turnovers are a mad scramble to wash linens, clean bathrooms, and mop or vacuum. So, schedule a quarterly deep clean for your short-term rental unit. This will give your housekeeper time to conduct a floor-to-ceiling cleaning, wash windows, clean appliances, dust ceiling fans, vacuum under beds and sofas, remove wall scuffs, and inventory anything he or she may need from you to help keep your space sparkling clean. Cleanliness is the number one way to impress your guests, so do not hesitate to invest in deep cleaning.

→ Chapter 13 Takeaways ←

- Review all guest reviews, both public and private, to understand what to repair and add to your space for optimal guest satisfaction.
- Consider using some of the revenue generated from your short-term rental to fund additional amenities and renovations that will add value to your space and guest stays.
- Conduct quarterly owner's eye inspections and schedule quarterly deep cleanings to stay abreast of any property issues, repairs, or organizational needs that require attention.

14. OPTIMIZE YOUR EARNING POTENTIAL

As you continue on your short-term rental journey and transition from starting your listing to maintaining your listing, the goals and best practices for search rank placement discussed in Chapter 11 are still important. You will also need to adjust your pricing mindset in order to continue to grow your listing's revenue. As a host, you should continue to monitor and optimize your listing's ranking in search results. This can be done manually or through the use of a software tool such as Rankbreeze.

Optimizing Your Listing for Rank

To manually monitor your listing's rank placement, start by activating *Incognito* or *Private* browsing mode in your computer's search browser. This disables any cookies Airbnb has placed on your browser that might skew your search results. Next, navigate to the Airbnb website and enter the location of your listing. Select check-in and check-out dates that correspond with your next available/open weekend. Select four guests, and then click the search button. Record the placement of your listing as compared to others shown on the results page. Your goal is to always be on page one of search results, preferably as near to the top as possible.

Consider changing the number of guests in your search criteria to two and six. You may be surprised by the results. Record these results as well. If you have a four-bedroom property, you should notice that it ranks lower for two guests than for six. The Airbnb algorithm is very clever and is striving to show each future guest group the most appropriate listing for their group size. Create a spreadsheet to record the dates and search results for groups of two, four, and six.

A more automated way to monitor your search rank placement is to use a software tool such as Rankbreeze. This software performs the same process as a manual search and does so daily, recording your listing's rank for the range of one guest through your maximum allowed occupancy number. The advantage to this automated analysis is that instead of a brief snapshot of one date, you receive daily results in graphs/charts similar to the one below.

Image from RankBreeze Calendar Rankings

www.rankbreeze.com

The Rankbreeze chart displays your exact rank placement for your next six open booking windows. As a host, I find this exceptionally valuable. If you find that your listing is consistently ranking in the number one or two positions, this is great news and indicates that you are excelling as a host. Your ranking also yields the opportunity to flex your listing authority by beginning to raise your nightly base rate. Proceed with caution. I suggest increasing your base rate in PriceLabs by $10 and monitoring your rank placement over the next month to see how this price change affects your rank placement. Repeat this process monthly until you find an equilibrium between rank placement and base rate price that feels comfortable to you.

If you learn that your listing is placing low in search results and showing in the thirtieth, fiftieth, or hundredth spot, do not panic. This information is good to know and signals that you need to start making changes. Remember, what gets measured gets managed. Start by checking your price relative to your competition for the available dates that you are ranking poorly. You can do this manually or using software tools, as Rankbreeze has a *Details* link that shows each of your competitors' prices for a given booking window. If your listing is priced higher than better-ranked listings, consider lowering your price for that specific date range in PriceLabs. This approach affords you the ability to laser target near-term price reductions that will lead to higher occupancy.

If your pricing is in line with your competition and your listing is still ranking poorly, it is time to reoptimize your listing. The reoptimization process involves taking a detailed look at each of the components listed below. We have outlined how most successful hosts treat each of these areas. Ask yourself: "Have I really done my very best to follow all of the best practices for each listing component?" It is very common to not go "all in" in every area as a new host. Perhaps you skimped on professional photos or did not get around to implementing a dynamic pricing tool or automated messaging software. If your listing is not showing on the first page of an Airbnb search, then your listing is essentially invisible, which will cause your bookings to suffer. It is well worth your time to systematically review, improve, and update each of the components listed in order of importance below, with the goal of reducing booking friction and making your listing more enticing and accessible to guests.

- Instant booking
- Dynamic pricing
- Superhost status
- Calendar open twelve months
- Cancellation policy
- Pet friendly
- Minimum night stay
- Cleaning fee
- Listing title and description
- Cover photo and photo arrangement
- Amenities review
- Listing setup details
- Reviews analysis

The first short-term rental investment Danielle and I made was a condo in the Turks and Caicos Islands. We had successfully rented the place for years. The COVID-19 pandemic temporarily halted international travel, and our condo bookings suffered. We anticipated that as travel rates rose, our booking rates would increase in correlation. It turns out we were wrong. Our bookings did not come back, and we began to wonder why.

RankBreeze revealed to us that our condo listing was buried below 199 other listings on Airbnb. Knowing about our terrible ranking, we immediately wanted to change our pricing. However, minimum base pricing is set by the resort where our condo is located, so we did not have the option to lower our prices, even by $10 a night. This pricing paralysis forced us to consider other ways to optimize our listing.

We logged into our Airbnb host account and noticed new amenity toggles that could be switched to *On* for the condo. Next, we changed our cancellation policy to be more lenient. Then, we took stock of the key amenities of our condo and resort. We asked ourselves the question, "What made our place better than other island condos?"

This exercise was very helpful and led us to change our listing title to include "On-Site Spa." We also changed the sequence of our photos to emphasize the pool, beach, and hot tub instead of the interior of our condo. Finally, Danielle updated our condo listing description to emphasize our amenities, family-friendliness, and our high level of guest communication around custom recommendations for restaurants, activities, and excursions.

The result of our listing reoptimization efforts materialized overnight. RankBreeze identified that our condo listing had skyrocketed from number 200 in Airbnb search to number 2! This illustrates how important it is to monitor and adjust your listing. It also shows how sensitive the Airbnb algorithm is to listing changes. Consider putting an alert in your calendar every two months to remind you to check your listing status and make any necessary tweaks in order to stay at the top of your market. Optimizing your listing every two to three months is essential to staying ahead of your competitors on the Airbnb platform. Understanding this concept and properly executing it will put you in the top 1 percent of all hosts.

Adjusting Your Pricing to Balance Revenue and Occupancy

At this point, you should be well on your way to Superhost status, and your listing should be generating a solid stream of bookings. When you established your initial base rate in PriceLabs, it was priced just below your market average. It is now time to reevaluate this base price using the lens of your upcoming occupancy. As previously mentioned, the goal is 100 percent near-term occupancy, 50 percent occupancy or greater over the upcoming thirty days, and 25 percent occupancy or greater sixty days out. If you are meeting or exceeding these goals and your listing is ranking well, it is time to begin systematically increasing your base rate in PriceLabs.

If your property has high occupancy and high search rank position, begin your rate increase by adjusting your base rate to the average base rate for your market or slightly higher than the average rate. Once you have made the price change, evaluate occupancy and search rank over the next thirty days. If after a price increase your listing continues to maintain high occupancy and high search rank position, continue to increase your base price each month by $10–15 per night. Your listing will grow in authority as you continue to cultivate 5-star reviews and wish list additions. Over the coming months and years, your base rate has the capability of increasing, tempered only by your rank placement and occupancy as measured against the thirty- and sixty-day occupancy targets.

> **Pro Host Tip:** Consider using the "Help me choose my base price" function in PriceLabs. It makes base pricing suggestions calculated by comparing your listing's performance relative to competitors in your market.

In addition to base rate increases, there are several other strategies for maximizing your revenues. A good place to start is with the shoulder nights of Thursday and Sunday. In my experience, popular dynamic pricing tools do a great job of differentiating midweek demand from weekend demand and setting prices accordingly. However, as your listing's weekend prices get higher, guests will begin to game the system by opting for Thursday to Friday stays or Saturday to Sunday stays to avoid your high weekend rates. To account for this consumer behavior, set a *Night of the Week* adjustment in PriceLabs for Thursday and Sunday nights. I apply a 15 percent price increase to all Thursday and Sunday nights. By systematically raising the price of shoulder nights, you will increase revenue generated by your short-term rental.

Another strategy for maximizing revenue is to charge extra guest fees. Your pricing should be appealing to couples or couples with a child, but as the guest count increases, so should your rates. This is both fair to you as the host as you will incur additional expenses for additional guests, and it is equitable for larger groups who have the ability to share accommodation fees. I recommend setting an extra guest fee of $20 per night for groups larger than three. In this scenario a party of six would pay an extra $60 per night to book your property.

Optimizing Minimum and Orphan Night Stays

Many hosts are curious what the "right" number is for minimum night stays. Decades ago, most vacation rental owners or managers required a full, weeklong, Saturday to Saturday booking. In today's travel culture, requiring a seven-day minimum booking is not advisable. I recommend setting a two-night minimum stay for your short-term rental.

Allowing two-night stays minimizes your "orphan nights" which are single-night stays caught between two bookings. For example, you may have one set of guests book a Monday and Tuesday night stay and another set of guests book a Thursday and Friday night stay within the same week. In this scenario, Wednesday becomes an orphan night. I would prefer to have one night open in a calendar than three or four nights orphaned due to greater minimum night requirements.

There are three ways to handle orphan nights. First, you can reach out to the guests on either side of the orphan night and ask them if they would like to extend their stay through the orphan night date for an attractive price. Using Hospitable for all of my standard guest messages gave me the idea to have a standard message to pitch orphan nights. While I cannot use the software to automate the sending of the message, I have a saved message in Airbnb that I send to guests staying on either end of an orphan night or nights. Sending this message helps keep my calendar full and the Airbnb algorithm happy.

My Orphan Night Email Template

> Please let me know if I can be of any assistance as you plan your
> trip. Also, we have an unexpected opening the night of October
> 28. If you have any inclination to extend your stay, this night
> could be made available at an attractive rate.

A second option is to set your PriceLabs tool to override your
Airbnb minimum night setting and allow one-night bookings only in
orphan night situations. Remember, you are striving for maximum
occupancy, so if you end up charging less to book an orphan night,
you are still reaping rewards from the Airbnb algorithm.

> Side note: I personally set PriceLabs to allow one-night bookings
> for orphan nights at my two-bedroom cabins. I do not allow
> one-night bookings at my larger three- or four-bedroom listings.
> Why? The larger the space, the more likely someone will want
> to rent it for a one-night party.

The third way to handle an orphan night is to use it for yourself.
You could go to enjoy the area, but as a host, it is vital to be vigilant
about your property condition. Spending an evening in your place
will give you time to reorganize cupboards, find and make small
repairs, and update your list of items to replace and amenities to add.

Another way to leverage your stay during an orphan night is
to actively work to be a good neighbor. As a short-term rental host,
you want to keep on the good side of your immediate neighbors and
community in case of guest emergencies, natural disasters, or changing
community by laws about short-term rentals. Get to know your
neighbors during orphan stays. Ask if there are any community dues,
ask how to donate to any road improvement funds, and consider
conducting a roadside trash pickup. Your good intentions will be

noted by the community and will keep you in good standing.

In summary, the more you can stay at your property on orphan nights, the better your listing will perform. As a host, you will constantly find things to fix, organize, and improve. Incremental maintenance you do will keep your listing pristine and your guests 5-star review-happy. You will also learn more about the area your property is located in, so that you can give better recommendations to your guests.

Social Media Marketing

Are you active on Facebook, Instagram, Pinterest, or TikTok? If so, take the opportunity to share your new property with your friends and followers. If you are curious about one or more of these social platforms, now may be the time to dive in and learn what they are all about. Social media is not going away, and our target guest audience is consuming more content on social media than ever before.

Many purchase decisions begin on social media, as more people use these platforms instead of a Google search. As a host, you have already invested time and money, acquired photography, written copy, and researched activities close to your short-term rental. Why not use the content and photos you have accumulated to promote your property? You can use your existing social media accounts or create new business accounts dedicated to promoting your listing(s). Be sure to link all of your posts to your Airbnb listing so that viewers can instantly find and book your space.

Creating a Custom Web Page for Your Listing

Building a custom website for your property or properties is a great way to showcase your listing or your entire investment portfolio. Once again, you already have photos, copy, and research to repurpose on your website. Tools such as Strikingly or Wix require no coding skills and make building a custom website easy and affordable. I do not recommend accepting bookings from your website.

Instead, link your website directly to your Airbnb listing to drive more views and potential bookings of your space. The Airbnb algorithm tracks social media links to your listing, so more links will result in higher rank placement.

It is also smart to consider adding a blog to your site so that you can create posts about the property and about nearby activities and attractions. Have you ever wanted to be a restaurant critic or travel writer? Now is your chance! Any blog posts you write will be indexed by Google. This means that individuals searching for the best restaurants or things to do in your market area can find and read your blog and, by association, they will see and hopefully book your Airbnb listing.

Paid Advertising

Investing a small amount of monthly revenue into a paid advertising budget can significantly boost your website and social media exposure. Facebook, Instagram, and Pinterest ads are relatively simple to create and direct toward potential guests.

You can choose to focus your advertising within a certain mile radius of your listing and target viewer interests, such as hiking, mountain biking, and skiing. You can also target any major nearby attractions, such as national parks or wineries. Targeting your ads in this way allows social media platforms to show your ads to the people most likely to be looking for an Airbnb in your area based on their location and interests. This means you are not wasting your advertising dollars showing ads to individuals who are not likely to book your space.

We allocate approximately $100 per month to paid advertising. Whether it brings in new bookings or simply boosts our listings' views and ranking, it is money well spent. Be aware that first-time advertisers can typically qualify for free advertising credits on the majority of social media platforms. It is a great way to try out your ideas and finetune your ad focuses.

→ Chapter 14 Takeaways ←

- Monitor your listing rank on Airbnb, make adjustments to your pricing, listing photos, cancellation policy, etc., to boost your listing to the first page of search results for your area.
- Balance your short-term rental revenue and occupancy through price adjustments and guest fees. Your goal is to charge the highest rental rates possible while maintaining 95 percent occupancy.
- Adjust minimum-night stay requirements to minimize orphan nights between bookings.
- Consider investing in social media marketing and paid advertising to drive more interest and traffic to your short-term rental.

→ Tools & Technologies ←

RankBreeze is a tool that allows hosts to track their listing position in Airbnb search results so they can optimize their rank and visibility.

15. GROWING YOUR PORTFOLIO, CONVERTING LONG-TERM RENTALS, AND REPURPOSING UNDERUTILIZED SPACES

Your first short-term rental investment has been listed, optimized, and is now paying out the dividends you were looking for. Now what? Now is a great time to consider your second investment property. What is better than one cash-generating property? Two or more!

If you love the area where your current short-term rental property is located, start looking at other properties for sale in this market. In this scenario, the second property is almost always easier to find than the first. You will be familiar with the area amenities and neighborhoods, and you already have a trusted real estate agent. You have built a support team and have operational systems in place. In short, you are now a fully operational short-term rental investor.

Create your portfolio growth strategy with quality of life and financial wellbeing in mind. You want to invest more to make more, but you also want to have time to live your *Why* and enjoy your life. Adding two new properties per year is a very manageable and realistic goal. Do not forget to factor in the time you will spend on continuous micro improvements for your current property. Maintaining quality of properties and quality of life are critical to your success as a short-term rental host.

As your portfolio grows to eight or ten properties, you may wish to hire a full-time assistant or part-time virtual assistant to handle day-to-day communications. This may free you to indulge in more free time or pursue additional investments. We are seeking quality of life and financial independence through real estate, which may come at the expense of some marginal or incremental profit. You will find your way, and your way may change over time. It may swing like a pendulum during various times in your investment career.

Warning: Do not let your newly gained Airbnb knowledge lead to overly aggressive investing! Looking at revenue potential and listing opportunities in your area can make planning to add three or four new properties per year to your portfolio seem plausible. If you are the person responsible for the majority of renovations, repairs, decorating, guest relations, and listing optimization, adding too many properties too quickly can result in a nightmare.

If you would like to diversify your short-term rental portfolio, it is time to start looking for a new market. Refer back to Chapter 4 and refresh your knowledge about the best practices for identifying viable rental markets in any given area. While you will still be able to leverage the majority of your knowledge garnered from your first investment, you will most likely need to build a new dream team to support your new one.

A benefit to investing in multiple markets is that you are insulating yourself from area-specific adversity. Should one market begin passing legislation that makes hosting difficult or experience a natural disaster such as a forest fire or red tide, not all of your investments will be affected.

During the beginning of the COVID-19 pandemic, the majority of my properties experienced a short-term rental ban mandated by one county. County officials were trying to decrease virus spread by limiting new visitors to the area. I am uncertain how effective this effort was, but it certainly put me in a tough spot as a host. Having the ability to continue renting my properties in other counties, as well as pivoting to thirty-day or longer rentals in order to be compliant with the ban kept me in the black. Diversification over multiple areas can protect you from a similar scenario.

Converting Long-Term Rentals

Do you currently own a long-term rental property? Now may be the perfect time to explore converting it into a short-term rental. You will make triple the revenue and have way fewer occupant headaches.

I coach a retired couple who had purchased a historic farmhouse with the intention of renovating it into a long-term rental. They were new to the area, but the Gates were the previous owners of forty long-term rentals in California. I talked to them about the possibility of short-term rentals, and they completely changed their plan for the farmhouse.

The Gates were familiar with long-term rentals and quickly understood the exponential increase in revenue that a short-term rental offered them. I admire their ability to pivot to something new. Guess what? The Gates love working on this fresh venture together. They are excited about surprising and delighting their guests, and they are thrilled to have a space friends can use when visiting for a week. Creating a short-term rental has enriched their retirement experience, as well as their bank account.

Do not miss out on the opportunity to convert your long-term rental. You will enjoy how pleasant and happy you make the majority of your guests. Instead of having to complete major renovations after a multi-year tenant moves out, you will execute micro updates monthly. It is an entirely different investment that will return much higher revenues and provides a much better investor lifestyle.

Mixing Short-Term Rental Units into Multi-Family Investments

If you currently own a multi-family unit in a desirable location, there are many reasons to contemplate converting a few units into short-term rentals. Consider some of the following benefits to a mixed-use investment:

- Having a clean, well-designed, fully furnished "show" unit will close long-term leases faster while attracting a higher-caliber renter.
- Expose your properties to a wider audience. It is better than free advertising
- Gain two to three times monetary returns on the same investment property.
- Diversify your income streams.
- Add new skills to your investing and team toolkit.
- Understand your product better. Short-term guests are programmed to provide honest immediate feedback about the quality of their stay
- Observe firsthand what is happening at your properties from an operations and tenant perspective.
- Show potential investors and partners that you are future-focused and know how to stand out from the crowd.
- Create a new way to generate cash flow from idle inventory with a minimal investment in furnishings and photography.
- Attract corporate clients and mobile workers looking for short to mid-term furnished rentals.
- Harness the rental arbitrage. Airbnb professionals are leasing units to run as short-term rentals and generating large returns.

Repurposing Underutilized Spaces

The explosion of demand for short-term rentals means that you can generate revenue by repurposing unusual spaces, not just apartments or homes. If you peruse Airbnb listings, you will see teepees, boats, and airstreams available for nightly rental. There is a portion of the population that delights in staying in atypical locations. My wife is one of them.

I am in the midst of coaching a couple as they convert a garage office in downtown Wilmington into an Airbnb. After the COVID-19 pandemic struck, Lindsay's design company employees were all working from home, and the office space was sitting vacant. A client connected us, and we were able to create a quick plan to convert the office space into a super cool Airbnb. Our plan will move this couple from a situation in which they are paying a mortgage on an empty office to one in which they are generating monthly income through their new, hip Airbnb space. If you are in a similar situation, be sure to call your county building authority to check the local zoning ordinances that relate to use of space. You can also reach out to the local planning/development office to better understand if there are any restrictions or necessary permits for short-term rentals.

With whatever space you own, there is the potential to convert it into a short-term rental property. Let go of any self-limiting beliefs that are holding you back. Fate and Airbnb reward the creative, so get out there and get started.

Alternative Properties and Land Development

Short-term rental properties are not limited to traditional homes or cabins. If you own land you might want to consider adding an alternative property such as a tiny home, tiny mobile home, Airstream trailer, yurt, teepee, geodesic dome, or a tree house. There are many benefits to alternative properties. Many times they are less expensive and take less time to construct than a traditional home. There is also the "cool factor" associated with alternative properties. If you conduct a Google search for the most wish-listed Airbnb stays, you will find they are listings for unique spaces. Alternative properties appeal to a large portion of guests looking for an exciting or unusual stay, which is one more way to stand out from other Airbnb properties in your market.

If you are purchasing or building an alternative dwelling try to design and position the property to maximize sunrise and sunset. Guests enjoy sitting on a porch with coffee at sunrise and viewing sunset from a back deck or balcony. Handicap access is another amenity to consider adding to your design. Adding a ramp, removing any entry stairs, or building an ADA-compliant bathroom can make your listing incredibly attractive to the multitude of guests with limited mobility.

During a window of time when Danielle and I were unable to find a cabin to purchase, we bought several wooded lots throughout our market. The plan for this land is to build traditional cabins, or alternative properties. Land development is a multi-step endeavor. Before purchasing land with the intention of building an investment property, you will need to determine some basic things. It may seem daunting to find the answers to all of these questions, but they are important for you as an investor to understand the scope of the project, its timeline, and cost.

Land Development Questions to Ask and Answer:

- Is the land zoned for residential construction and short-term rental use?
- Does the land have access to a sewer system or will you need to investigate septic systems?
- Does the land "perk" for a specific number of bedrooms (ie, will the soil work with a traditional septic drain field)?
- Is the land in a flood zone?
- Are there plans for nearby land, such as a wind farm or landfill, that would make the area unsuitable for a short-term rental property?
- What permits need to be filed for pulling electric, connecting to sewer, excavating, and building?

- What inspections need to be scheduled before, during, and after building?
- How much will inspections cost?
- How much will surveying the land cost?
- How much will architectural drawings cost?
- How much will installing a septic system (if necessary) cost?
- How much will ground preparation and grading cost?
- How much will building materials and labor cost?
- What is the timeline for surveying, inspections, architectural drawings, installing septic or sewage systems, preparing the land for building, and building the structure?

Depending on the state and county you are investing in, prices and timelines can vary exponentially. Personally, as Danielle and I explored the variables associated with building we determined that placing a temporary structure on the land was the best choice for us. We are in the midst of preparing one lot with panoramic views as the site for a geodesic dome. Danielle loves how creative she can be with furnishings and landscaping. I appreciate that the dome is inexpensive and will create cash flow to save for building a cabin for this location in the future.

→ Chapter 15 Takeaways ←

- Consider investing in a second short-term rental property to build your portfolio and accelerate financial freedom.
- If you own long-term rentals, weigh the option of converting them into short-term rentals for higher revenue potential.
- If you are a multi-family unit investor, consider turning a few units into short-term rentals.
- Consumer demand for unusual stays can make adding a teepee, building a geometric dome, or converting non-traditional dwellings into Airbnb listings a possibility worth exploring.

FAREWELL

You did it! You finished this book. You are now armed with the knowledge, tools, and systems needed to catapult yourself into short-term rental investing triumph. How do you summarize and share all that you have learned? We created the four pillars of short-term rental success to help you.

The Four Pillars of Short-Term Rental Success

1. Find Your Where
Pinpoint the location that makes the most sense for your short-term rental investment, using the advice and tools detailed in this book.

2. Make Your Listing Pop
Use paint, unique decor, and HDR photography to make your listing stand out.

3. Price for Occupancy
Implement dynamic pricing with the goal of 90 percent occupancy each month.

4. Optimize for Rank
As your short-term rental generates revenue, begin to optimize for rank.

Knowledge without action is useless. You invested your money and time to buy this book and read it. Go take the necessary actions to reap returns on your investments! The time is now!

This book was written as a blueprint for short-term rental success. Just as an architect continuously references a blueprint to ensure a structure is built correctly, you should refer back to chapters that correlate with where you are in your journey as you create your short-term rental. This will keep you on track to attain the financial freedom necessary to live a life you love.

We cannot wait to hear your success story!

If you need coaching or further guidance,
please send us a note at culin_danielle@hostcoach.co
or share your journey with us on Instagram at @host_coach.

Anyone can do it.
Not everyone will. Will you?

— Gary Keller

APPENDIX 1
Cabin Manual Example

Welcome to Our Cabin

Cabin WiFi

Our Wi-fi network is Mountain Wifi.

Connect using the password: youguestedit.

*If you're having trouble, please let me know ASAP via Airbnb chat. The previous guests may have consumed the data package and I can re-up it.

Gas Fireplace Instructions

First, make sure the gas is not turned off. Behind the fireplace you will see a flexible pipe with a small value running into the back of the fireplace. Make sure that the valve is on. The handle should run parallel/in line with the gas line.

Next, open the small door at the base of the fireplace and note the gas control knob. Turn the knob to PILOT LIT and press and hold in. If it does not light, then try this again with a match or lighter held beside it. It should make a small flame. Once you see the flame, please continue to hold the knob in for at least 30 seconds. Once the pilot is burning, you can use the remote to turn on the fireplace. Please let me know if you have trouble with any of those steps. I'm happy to help!

Where to Grocery Shop

Super Walmart in Luray has a huge selection of groceries and wine/ beer. **Food Lion** in Luray is another good choice.

Luray Restaurants/Breweries

West Main Market is the perfect spot for gourmet made-to-order hot and cold sandwiches and soup. Their roast beef and bleu cheese sandwich is a family favorite.

Gathering Grounds has fantastic coffee, baked goods, breakfast and more.

The Valley Cork is a lovely spot to stop for wine and a cheese board.

The Mimslyn Inn restaurant has a very nice Sunday brunch and serves dinner on select evenings.

Triple Crown BBQ is a cute country roadside stand across from Walmart. Their BBQ is fabulous! Pick it up to go, or sit at one of their outdoor tables. *They tend to sell out by early evening, so try to go for lunch.

Anthony's Pizza is a hole in the wall Italian restaurant that makes some outstanding pizza and pasta. The Italian Combo is delicious, with generous helpings of lasagna and alfredo.

Hawksbill Brewery serves up a wide variety of local beers. Try the Hooray for Luray IPA. *The beer and atmosphere is very friendly, but no food is served. You can have pizza delivered to the brewery.

Local Activities

Our River Outfitters is a fantastic place to rent tubes, kayaks, or rafts. We highly recommend reserving your boat/float and time slot online ahead of time. Pack a cooler with food and beverages (if you're in a raft) and enjoy the county pleasure of floating down the Shenandoah River taking in the beauty around you.

Luray Caverns has not only caverns, but a garden maze, ropes course, and a number of small shops/museums to explore. *This is a year-round option, as the cave temperature perpetually stays at 60 degrees. In the summer and fall it is wise to purchase your tickets online ahead of your visit.

The Luray Rescue Zoo is our absolute favorite destination in Luray. You can call the owner Mark, and he will arrange to give you a behind the scenes tour complete with tiger feeding and porcupine petting for $25/person. We have guests tell us it was the best thing they did all year!

Warehouse Art Gallery is very cool, with everything from chairs made out of belts to local watercolours and pottery.

Luray Singing Tower is a 47 bell Taylor Carillon that was built in 1937. Free recitals are played based on the following schedule:

April & May: Saturday & Sunday at 3 PM
June—August: Tuesday, Thursday, Saturday & Sunday at 8 PM
September & October: Saturday & Sunday at 3 PM

Skyline Drive offers some of the most incredible views of all of Shenandoah. You can decide to drive North 40 minutes to the Thorton Gap entrance, or drive south 46 minutes to the Swift Run entrance depending on how you want to start your sightseeing loop.

APPENDIX 2
Host Coach Technology Stack

The software and tools I use to succeed as a short-term rental host and coach.

Market Research
Redfin—an online, map-based real estate search engine and real estate brokerage

AirDNA—a software that tracks the performance data of over 10 million vacation rentals to analyze occupancy rates, revenue, and pricing

PriceLabs Market Dashboard—a fully automated personalized dashboard to track vacation rental and Airbnb data in any market

Listing
Airbnb—an online marketplace for short-term rental properties and tourism activities

Dynamic Pricing
PriceLabs Dynamic Pricing—a data-driven, dynamic pricing tool that automates nightly pricing for short-term rentals to optimize rental revenue

Automated Messaging

Hospitable (formerly Smartbnb)—a software that centralizes and automates guest messaging through the Airbnb platform for one or multiple short-term rental properties

Cleaning Schedule

Google Sheets—a free online spreadsheet with the ability to be accessed and shared by multiple people and updated in real-time

Payments

Zelle—a mobile payment application that facilitates peer-to-peer money transfers without cash or bank visits

Bookkeeping

QuickBooks—an accounting software that helps manage invoices, expenses, pay bills and track cash flow

Optimization

RankBreeze—a tool that allows hosts to track their listing position in Airbnb search results so they can optimize their rank and visibility

Insurance

Proper Insurance—a company specializing in the insurance needs of short-term rental hosts

GLOSSARY

Algorithm—a process or set of rules to be followed in calculations or other problem-solving operations, especially by a computer

Application Programming Interface (API)—a software intermediary that allows two applications from different programs to talk to each other

Arbitrage—the process of purchasing an asset used for one purpose and repurposing it into another use for financial gain

Average Daily Rate (ADR)—a metric used in the hospitality industry to indicate the average revenue earned by a room or space in a given day

Bleisure—the practice of combining business travel and leisure travel into one trip

Bottom Line Revenue—a sales number showing the revenue generated in a given period of time after all expenses have been deducted

Financial Freedom—the status of having enough income to pay one's living expenses without having to be employed or dependant on others

Freestyle—the practice of driving through areas in search of properties not listed on traditional real estate sales platforms

Future Potential Guest (FPG)—an individual browsing Airbnb in search of accommodations

Gig Economy—a labor market with a prevalence of freelance work or short-term contracts instead of permanent jobs

High Season—the time of year when a place or area is most busy or booked

Low Season—the time of year when a place or area is least busy or booked

Macro Amenity—a large, positive property feature that most people do not have in their home or apartment, such as a screened porch, mountain views, hot tub, or river access

Micro Amenity—a smaller positive property feature, such as a hanging basket chair, fire pit, or teepee

Multiple Listing Service (MLS)—private databases that are created, maintained, and paid for by real estate professionals to facilitate their clients buying and selling property

Multi-Family Rental—a property containing three or more dwelling units

Magic Erasers—melamine sponge that micro sands surfaces to remove dirt, scuffs, and stains

Net Positive Cash Flow—when a business or investment has a surplus of cash after paying all operating costs

Orphan Night—a single open night between two bookings

Online Travel Agency (OTA)—a web-based marketplace that sell services related to travel, such as hotels, flights, and car rental companies

Page Rank—a value assigned to a listing as a measure of its popularity; used to determine the order in which Airbnb search results are presented

Self-Limiting Belief—beliefs that have the greatest potential to negatively impact you achieving your full potential

Short-Term Rental—a furnished, self-contained space that is rented for short periods of time; an alternative to hotel stays

Shoulder Night—the night on either side of a peak day of the week, such as Sunday

Shoulder Season—the time period between low season and high season

Search Engine Optimization (SEO)—the process of maximizing the number of visitors to a specific website by ensuring that site appears high on the list returned by a search engine

Top Line Revenue—a pure, gross sales number showing the revenue generated in a given period of time without expenses subtracted

Turnover—a day when guests check out and a property must be cleaned and made ready for new guests

Work-Away Trip—a trip planned for one to work in an alternate destination and then enjoy that area post workday

ACKNOWLEDGMENTS

Thank you to the family, friends, and unsuspecting bystanders who have been pulled into all of our short-term rental adventures. Additional thanks to Danielle's Aunt Lori for sharing her secret cabinet painting techniques. We are gratefully indebted to Ladd Gasparovic, Shannon Allan, and the entire Keller Williams family for hosting the presentation that spiraled into this book!

Every question, edit, and change suggested by our early peer reviewers helped transform *Host Coach* from a dream into a reality. We are endlessly grateful to: Sara Sackville, Michelle Bennett, Jackie Tate, Don Rowlett, Karen Rowlett, Jo Sackville, Lisa Tate, Phillip Marshall, Carl Engstrom, Valaerie Condict, and Aaron Daike, for their time, honesty, and contributions. Merric, thank you for keeping yourself busy as we wrote during evenings, weekends, and snow days. You are an amazing young man, and we cannot wait to read the books that you will write in your lifetime.

Deepest thanks to our professional support team for transforming our rough draft into a polished work that can help others succeed in short-term rental investing. Nicole Hall you are a wonder! Your patience, flexibility, and wordsmithing have done nothing but elevate our vision and execution of this book. Brin Stevens, thank you for making time for us in your busy schedule when there was none. You are a literary genius and we're so grateful to call you a friend. Vanessa Mendozzi, your creative concepts are perfection. Working with you for cover and interior layout design has been effortless. Thank you to our dear friend Kimberly Smith for cheerfully and endlessly editing book images. It is a true pleasure to have worked with female professionals throughout our writing process. A group champagne lunch is in order!

We are also thankful for God's hand in our lives, his blessings, abundance, and the ability to share our knowledge with others to make the world a better place.

Made in the USA
Monee, IL
10 November 2022

17507088R00127